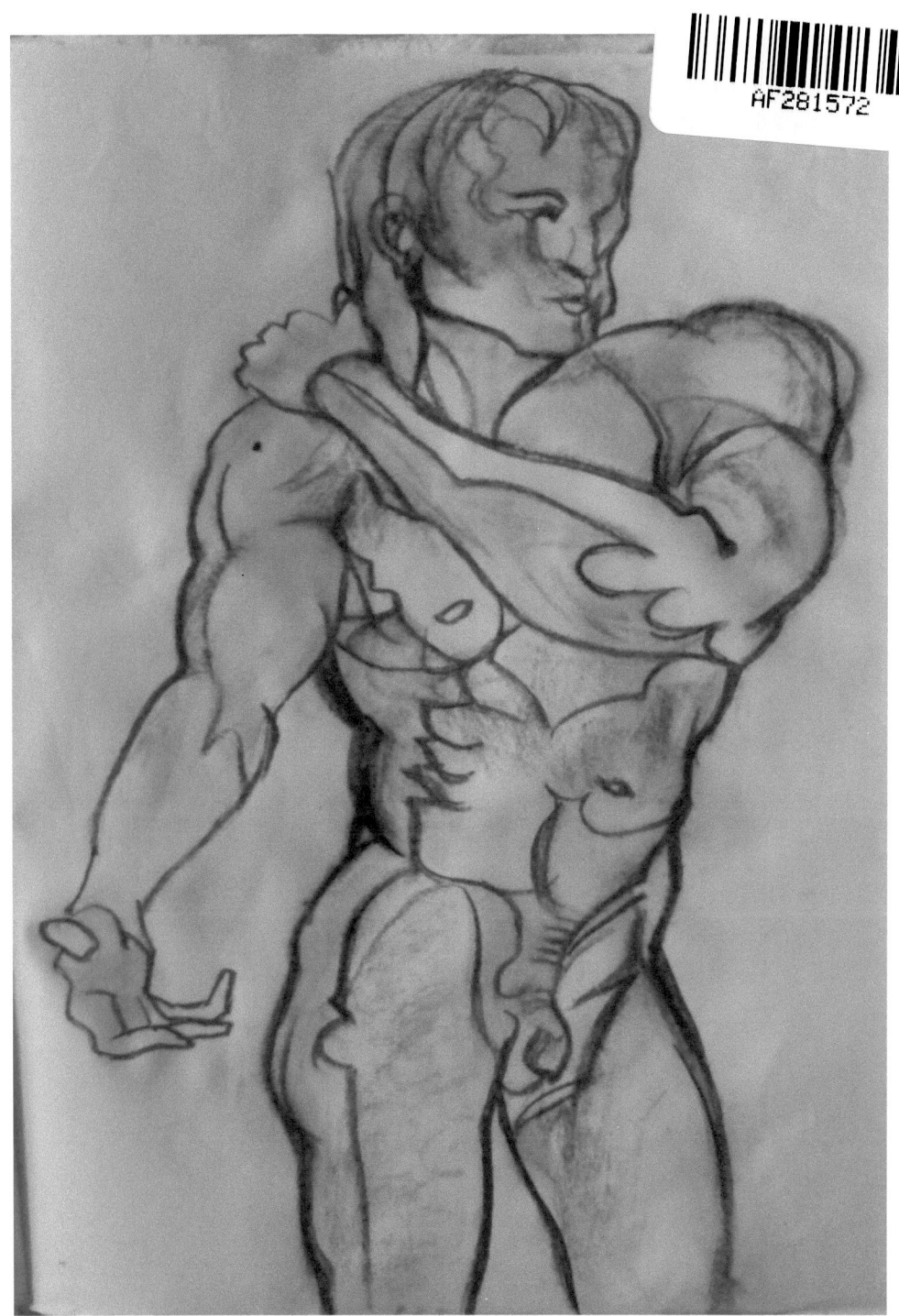

« *SAMSAARA* »

**There happen things,
when we have some good looking,
to the outside of the own transformation,
seeing the other side of the Atlantik,
read in the story of other lands.**

**You could start
to learn from another.**

Imprint

BoD - Books on Demand, Norderstedt ISBN 978-3-7597-5312-0

Here is

No space
for violence

against women !!

Heike Thieme – YLVA

Heike Thieme

Careful

with the
DATING TRAP !

Strictly speaking...
the voluntary performance of sexual favors
is like an emotional breaking of earthly laws,
high to being down to earth,
as guaranteed to be protective in its effect
and contradiction
as the parallel between
thinking, waiting, switching and laughing
to stop the torrent of crying !
Strictly missing sausages still in the fridge !
WE ARE ALL INTERCONNECTED !
I am going to tell that I love not a single one,
but I love universally,
that is the fact to be,
the greed and ownership of heart
is the opposite that is wannabe,
I am going to get used to it,
that letting go is the finest thing to do, has that fine,
and that style of gentle beings, to let grow !

« Heike Thieme – Ylva »

Of all diagnoses

"normality"

is the most serious,
because it leaves no hope !

INTRODUCTION

What is man's true hunger?

Perhaps it is the desire to emotionally
degenerate in the family at Christmas?

Does it mean to respond to someone in love that you are beating yourself
up? Perhaps it is to take on the other person's inferiority so that they feel
loved? Who is ignorant and stupid, all their actions stem from hurting
someone else with every act, especially the elderly, the weak and children,
that is, they kick someone down to show their superiority! Wouldn't the
mentally ill imitate this because they themselves are tired of life? Perhaps
they are unable to find peace under pressure from others and are able to pass
this aggression on to others?

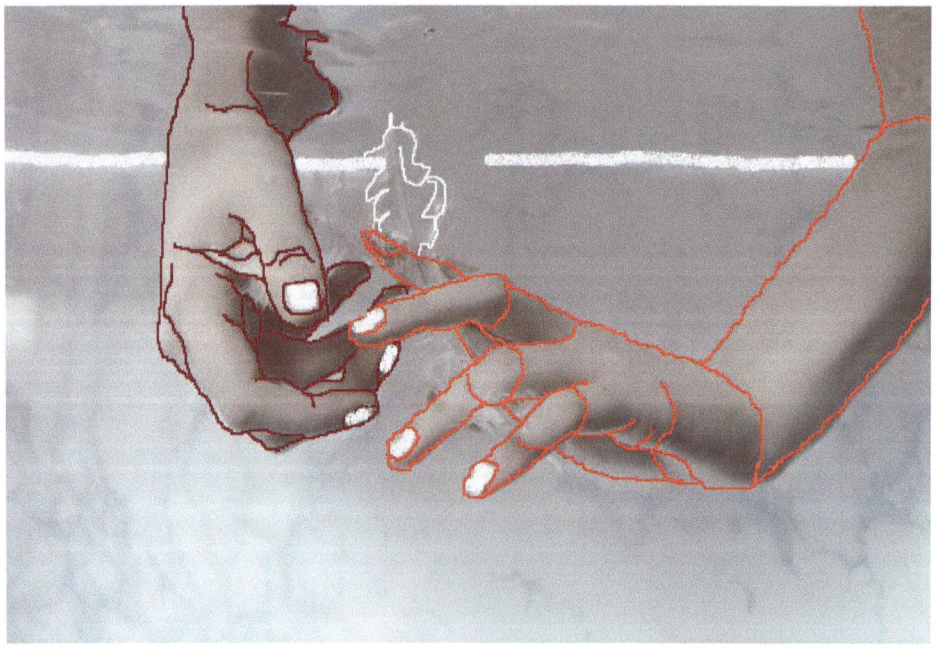

Because of all this complexity, perhaps women are so difficult to approach. Sometimes people face unforeseen circumstances in life, take for example the autistic father who can play the musical sounds and their beauty very well. He is unemployed. However, it is clear, I feel sympathy for him. He spoke in the following words:

"Heike I have said it before and I will say it again that I am very proud of your deep, unique strength, a great willpower and self-control, that is divine of you. You refuse to ever let anger rule in hard or provocative situations. You are absolutely right in your analysis of altruism. It has nothing to do with being rich or not, it comes entirely from within."

Awareness is the key to greatness. It is a leading path to attaining righteousness, although in the vast world of today both the common man and the rich and wealthy sometimes lack this fact because they lack awareness."

Expect nothing from anyone and you will never be disappointed. Meditation reaches your soul to your greatest heaven. Meditation is life, it is the way. the TAO. It brings the understanding of duality that you mentioned. You gave another beautiful explanation and I am still proud of you as always. At the end of your section you made me even prouder when you understood that there is no perfect man, we can only be close to perfection, maybe not even close because we all have at least 7 flaws which I know psychologically are more, this is true for every human being. No matter how hard we try to improve ourselves, life will always be interesting with the good, the bad and the ugly, through thick and ding, through evil and good, through smiles and tears and so on. This includes your statement to demonstrate understanding on a certain level.

If the man himself says,
"If I am the man who was one of those who treated women in such a hostile and miserable way, then I will NEVER be one of them!"

We live in an ambivalent Western world that simultaneously strives for progress, but is nevertheless based on the fact that this technological achievement or prosperity may have only been built on the backs of women who are still used, degraded, oppressed, humiliated, exploited and enslaved, badly treated people. Today I will still count myself among those women who have never entered into a partnership for these reasons.

I also did my best to keep my hands off the idea of marriage and will never do so in this country. Our country still lives in the Middle Ages when it comes to marriage.

No one ever said it would be easy, encourage and be encouraged. It's not that I'm a skeptic and don't believe anyone, I just prefer to see for myself. High standards protect you from inferior experiences.

It is the intellect that puts ideas in the form of thoughts and at the same time collects and organizes the thoughts. There are great ideas that are beyond the ordinary human mentality that can take all visible forms. These great ideas tend to descend. They want to manifest themselves in precise forms. These precise forms are the thoughts. And anyway, I think that is what is meant by intellect: it is it that gives the ideas the thought form.

Living with poor people out there on the streets and profiting from that image of being a tough guy and being in solidarity with them. But I am a woman with dignity who cares, so I care about myself too, never giving myself away for prostitution to get a famous image, and I know that there are men who do that too.

We are all human beings, male or female. We are born under a specific purpose, the echo of the Divine, for which I feel responsible myself.

No matter how hard we try to better ourselves, life will always be interesting with the good, the bad and the ugly, through thick and ding, through evil and good, through smiles and tears and so on. This includes your explanation to demonstrate understanding at some level. We all have hopes and dreams, keep believing that things will work out, one way or another, they will. Moments of physical solitude, times of meditative retreat are necessary, but they are subordinate and supportive. Acting as sadhana, as sacrifice to God, first without attachment to the results and then without attachment to the act itself, is the sine qua non.

Finding Prince Charming online is a common occurrence, and all end up as sad and painful to angry, many small-minded and reckless as egoists who have had their fun with it. I can really imagine how easily people are manipulated, then sexually abused, then reduced in their emotions.

This made fools of, used for other people's games and aggressions, spoiled and insulted again, and finally abandoned. I know people who credibly make victims of inexperienced people precisely because they themselves have no understanding of other people's feelings. And in my opinion, such behavior and people whose negativity is aggressive are missing out on a great insight into their own mental illness and should try to start healing from scratch instead of continuing. The more people act like this and grow old in their hearts and become hard, the longer they let the world feel it too. There are certain differences in how people approach old age, not everyone goes down this path with dignity! But I still want to witness such behavior in order to learn how others can be warned. I want to belong to the empath and the old soul and stay alive and save other lives.

I was never the best. I always had to work on myself. Anyone who learns to criticize themselves will later be seen as a whole person in their career. It is important not to always be dependent on someone else.

Once the anger bomb really gets going...
the friend is only seen as an enemy.

WHO BRINGS THE SUN INTO THE LIVES OF OTHERS,
WILL HAVE SUN IN HIS LIFE THE SAME !

It is some sort of ancient compass.
Yes, indeed ! It is always a good thing to do,
to find the orientation to our roots,
then travel to middle age, then travel to stone age,
then fly with an eagle's wings, the friends all live far,
we have to learn to fly to see them.

It gets to know the world independently. It speaks the languages of its
surroundings, and the mixture becomes substance. Complexity becomes
commonality, discovery becomes a created future. Understanding grows into
inner peace and existence grows into gratitude. His desire turns out to be an
ability to love and the urge to share it with others. So he experiences love as
a simple vehicle. And people see wisdom in this, it's all about gaining
experience.

I try to break the stone around my heart.
I forgive the Americans,
and I try another second time,
to dedicate one of my Big Books
as a sign from my heart,
to connect as friends, please for a long time,
that New Book is dedicated to You
Adam Michael Smith,
the one that i started to trust in real,
and i am i because of this,
that is truly a good good feel !
let the small boys pass,
let them run through their streets,
let now the Big Boys win !
Blessings from me,
Heike

Morning breakfast is always one apple,
have some fruits in the house, bake a little cake !
We all know eat an apple a day, keeps the doctor away !
that is truly to be seen, that those left docs won't be more of them, lesser and
lesser, all those poor people who know nothing about healing themselves
soon will find no docs anymore, i mean if people want to stay childish, and
wait still for the big bro telling how to come along, will end in a one way
street, as long as they keep on ignoring themselves.

Remembering my birth
that of my Sonboy,
meanwhile i shouted out loud
all way long eight hours,
in a power that those clouds
in summer never dared to appear,
hahaha
really that one of my Son's father,
he would as watcher
really not have survived,
hahaha think of it now 27 years after
funny !

I advise against consultants
whose salaries are useful for,
the advisors on corruption in politics,
which serve to clear away tax money,
the corrupt politicians themselves call their "victims",
who pay billions for their "advice", so the population pays,
they call it their drunken "kick", and they fall for politics,
they are their everyday "gags"
they are already taking anti-laughing pills,
that goes up like a hiccup,
comparatively slower in the economy,
and yet actually old hat !

Getting married today,
is like a sparrow in the hand,
instead of the pigeon on the roof,
everyone has already experienced this,
to have been left standing beforehand.
The romance thing is no more,
good if the woman's father was asked before,
then for the good reason
the woman was sold off like a commodity.
The most tasteless celebration of marriage
indicates the most tasteless marriage,
later no dress will fit anymore,
but the wrinkles on the face fit,
Letting go shortly after,
to save your own face,
to let him/her go !

Work for women today:
housework in marriage,
look out the cleaned window,
in love, then have children,
end up as a retired couple,
like Cinderella in the Mouse Tower,
you became intelligence, beauty, subtlety
reduced to a couch potato,
Outside, Mr. "Papa's" successor could
killing dragons on the battlefield,
her life never resembled an adventure,
just become a new "possession"....
it is often said,
"If we have nothing more to say to each other anyway,
We can finally get married!"

The breeze at dawn have secrets to tell you.
Don't go back to sleep!
You must ask for what you really want. Don't go back to sleep!
People are going back and forth
across the doorsill where the two worlds touch.
The door is round and open. Don't go back to sleep!

Small bill...doesn't particularly work for the woman,
I had while single parenting of unpaid working hours,
about those not provided by the city amounts for housing benefit,
with two under – respectively unpaid jobs, for the top-up pension,
which the employment office gave me without further ado forced,
for housework:
29 hours / week, plus the jobs, in unpaid forced labor
40 hours / week
...... a man would be willing to volunteer for just 20 hours!

The promise "Everything that is mine is also yours!" LIE!
The idea of getting married is a traditional understanding of roles
that is outdated!
In Germany it is not recommended not to plan a marriage
without first seeking legal advice about your future!
The women leave each other wrongly
when it comes to financial questions, turn to men.
Women earn less.
Marriage is not a division of property.
Afterwards the housewife only has the vacuum cleaner,
in their simplicity, the sheer good faith,
in good times and bad, hahaha,
but what she hasn't worked for doesn't belong to her.
Marriage in the country runs as a "community of gain".
He who earns money retains ownership alone.
The housewife asks for what she needs every week.
This hierarchy means that the earner alone has the say.

Whoever has the money can decide on purchases and expenses, manage the inheritance, expand the property, accumulate and spend, even go bankrupt, and does not have to account for it. More than 7% of women between 30-37 don't even have their own account. The woman who relies beautifully on her husband, are pretty stupid, they ask for household money, and have to get paid for their sex and services. So the idea of getting married is a trivial idea, But you can't buy anything from an idea! And setting aside and lying also says, to be completely financially exposed even in marriage, is to fall victim to a simple calculation !

In Germany it says: "Whatever loves each other does not share."
the only option his achievement in life to manage yourself as a woman, and to save his fortune, that you work for, people - is the divorce !

Families produce farts and mucus for the brain
They want a challenge cup the fart slime known from grandma's recipe
the title your dude for all situations they let it grow and pay you
They don't let you play, though, but do you buy every dude from them,
you have the opportunity and come into play
you can like the old aunt at the hole in the world
visit the desert with her, there you can count your pennies
and fall onto Ariele's mermaid bed
your next dude is hereby paid in advance, photograph the hero at the rodeo
see the family joy at seeing you as fireworks on the flat screen
sink in and clean the aunt's toilet you can ride the bull in the pub
and take photos of the testicles under the truck
when the tenth burger comes out of your throat
check your recipes to find out how to do it
Meanwhile, Aunt Mann is in the Vietnamese brothel
so you can invite the millionaire's son
Long story short, what the aunt wants to give you
is only self-storage is enough, and on behalf of everyone in the family,
"NEVER SEE YOU AGAIN !"
Just one short insight about my family !

I had to play in the big golf before both kids with us play three times
" A Hole in One ", then tell my aunt twice she can "Fuck off" continue to
shout out, and forbid my wording, then my son catched a ball to the
publicum at the National Day's Rodeo, and i found one wonderful birds
huge feather, and told my aunt she is a coward, then at last at the airport, i
just told her "She may better care in future for her dog, and not like that
Godmother to my son !" and gave her from home my best new seven novels
as remembering present and her remind to her cheap english she speaks.
She really had to say "Thanks". I played the three "Hole in One" alone !

Die deutsche Tante hatte sich wirklich bei mir zu "bedanken".

I know, I am a woman in Germany.
I don't know an expensive life. That's why they want to prostitute me.
I'm trying to get work, but they suggest another business to me.
I'm solid and single, raising alone,
That's why I'm being chased into unemployment.
I am unbending. That's why I'm insulted and excluded.
I'm not one to spread my legs,
That's why I'm not suitable for a German marriage.
I'm not begging, but was always looking for work,
That's why I was bullied out of the apartment.
I'm often at home, I don't eat meat. That's why I just lie there.

Well, yes, it's reprehensible,
as a woman in Germany, and misunderstood !
80% people in Germany are dissatisfied with our bosses.
What are our bosses doing wrong?
That even recently in the series add the doctors to the strikers,
clearly also their skills, knowledge, studies
becomes an unfair means of enrichment abused by company owners,
whose healing art is unused, but wasted on cosmetic surgery,
with those in need standing outside.
Our country is watching and deliberately closes the hospitals.

Heike Thieme

La Limasse mystique

Weeste watt so no, Value-oriented foreign policy,
and child-friendly picture book theory,
and denouncing manner, massively maternally proselytizing,
almost abusive towards the youth, also plays with politics
"Madam" playing the "Lord," who wants to feel called that,
slightly crazy, as if imitated by sick people,
who are seen as neighborly and prone to aggression,
but hindered in their own perception,
not even a step in front of their "supervisors".
would venture into the basement...TSCHA people,
if you want to be incapacitated, should she go vote !

Whose ego has grown so far,
that he only does it for himself,
executes the evildoer for his guilt,
seriously just to fight the demons,
and to feel peace for once,
has moved away from what is a human duty,
crossing a red line.
Whose conscience, however,
precisely from doing it for eighty years,
he is related to me and a hero.
If I had someone today that I would love so much,
then I would advise him not to love me back,
because sometimes I feel through my experiences
like being put through a meat grinder.
blessings from my danish Uncle,
whose name is "Ernst Thieme", ernst means seriously.

If only now doctors etc.
go on strike instead of leaving empty-handed...
can I understand that, just look like a bungler,
only as a hired hand for humbug,
Doctors are not celebrities
Anyone who works in the system knows it
Prejudices only marry a rich doctor,
travel halfway around the world for him,
just the smart choice brought the one bursting with love
BACKFISCH finally under the hood,
Medicine was only worth it for the BACKFISH,
and choosing smart is how
"Open your eyes when choosing a career!"
I gave up forty years ago, duh!

NEVER AGAIN - IT'S RIGHT NOW!
Dirty Nazis used to say:
"When our opponents say, we got you before, given freedom of opinion !"
and Goebbels continued:
"Yes, you...us, that's not proof, we should give it to you too,
the right you gave us that is proof of that, how stupid you are !"

I KNOW WHY I'M NOT GETTING MARRIED!

When you sleep at night with your mouth open,
and the flies fall dead from the ceiling, and the woman says:
"Sleep on the couch in the living room!"

With the argument, "Only a Mett roll with onions can do that !"
You don't need a quickie for bad breath.

When I'm lying around like that
in the coffin and always wondering
how long I lie here like this, and death doesn't like me,
I ask myself too, as if it didn't make sense
to become immortal without further ado,
that the world lives in peace, them the lovely peace not to give at all,
that their world lives in peace...
I'm not a long-legged gazelle, those on the unicycle crossed the jungle,
and talks about bad and good people, to then stroke the bald heads,
and about their bald dogs to go a long way !
I DON'T THINK OF IT !
As a WOMAN you say in this country,
Some things belong to Bavaria
ACTUALLY FORBIDDEN HIS MOUTH !
Just look at him, the Bavarian man who...raises a woman who he then....
with enjoyment before they move out into life
violently with hatred, root and branch
rams it into the ground just because he can?
Someone who trumpets political fairy tales,
but can't stop his mouth from agitating?
Who is as clever as a hawk rarely like that
who throws taxpayer money away to prevent laws?
Who represents an opposition to the country,
the country is legally planning to take away its rights?

PONDER - instead of PRAYING!

WANT TO KNOW - instead of MUST BELIEVE!

NO POLITICIANS - who hang crucifixes instead of sinks!

With the COMFORT - of believing people, misleaders!

SEDUCT - instead of convincing from science!

I'm actually a painter, the fact of a blue-haired one
female sick bully penetrated as already mentioned 10 ago,
I was forced to write my doctoral thesis,
they are now available in three languages,
but the wife on the part of the landlord,
to protect against violence according to the law,
Guys, this hasn't happened yet!
Lovely, kind regards to your feet!
uhhhhh yesterday we went to the woods....
there was all over a dive in light green
we just dirigated us to our small bench in the center
there i lay down, and just watch that young tree up to its top with all those
beautiful powerful lights of leaves and sun
and stayed so half an hour to heal and i healed again
it was mould weather, bit wet in the sky and warm,
but truly light full and no wind so this did keep off the other people, just on
the way back met one single good friend, he made me strong again
this time it was his turn to make me believe, that life must go, and he won.

I just go ahead and print that saying of me about my "Reading", my
"Understanding of my Art", and "The Human as such" in all in all 69 pages,
that is in german, english understandable, and for the new tone that i maybe
will meet in autumn again, he is russian, i translated it all in all into russian
language for him. To be highly active now, very much is happening, and did
and always will be. I see it has the saying and essence like one would call it
a work, that i really brought me the parts together started, sothat my private
little "doctors work" needed all in all to this comprimated thought 7 years, to
start any projects in life, meant to arrange i gave away from the old life,
cleaned the attic, the cellar, and home place, then put all the small working
toys and things to use to better find into that one here then the thought
project was free to start. Jou i find then, when i feel to be friend to someone,
then for EVER not like the other side, if i would have seen the worst things
in life, then i would become like them NEVER !
HEIKE THIEME - YLVA -

31

It is the woods calling. The look inside the trees leaves. The calm of his stump so long to the sky. We must go there lay down and just recover from all the work.

Klug ist, wer nur die Hälfte von dem glaubt, was er hört. Noch klüger, wer erkennt, welche Hälfte die richtige ist.

To be smart, who only knows the half of this he believes, what hearing. But even smarter, who realizes, which half of it is the right one !

Life is Life
and Love is Love
Life is not just wicked electricity,
but all is light energy.

He always wanted to be a crab,
he is still sad have no scorpio sting,
he is hungry but all feet step in emptiness,
his big wish was to be big and have big feet,
he has no guessing how is abonded kids be,
his crab from neighborhood his new love,
he can't count how to dance on eight legs,
i would call him "The One lost his number !"
Hitler dead, the 30th of May 1945 !
His nazi life poorness was quit,
that way a coward did !

I can assure you he was cryogenically frozen on a super-advanced U-Boot and transported to Buenos Aires - where he still is.
Yes, i am clear thinking you are right. Quiet desilusionairy but true.
With one less of the nazis grow five more. They still keep their laws for surpression. They just have nowadays more trouble
when to lock in common people away from street,
today is not so easy anymore.

My theory is One Nazi, has the sickness to be in love with his face, his ideal
to rule the world, never, but the one was never loved at all.

Kidding me ? Give a cat a bed, like a child ?
this is the right way to treat a child, not a cat !
yess, and i would even not..take two twins apart,
and say there is the one to survive,
and the other to die, like that is any animal no pet,
to play the role of a human child,
because it is otherwise the opposite,
the human learns to grow up when he understands his own nature,
when watched how to handle thisfrom the animal in a natural way,

blessings Heike !

A blue tarantula !
The sympathy of spider, to me is his many tryings in life,
steady on the move, take one step and another step,
never win or loose weight, but stay to go on and on,
never push nor hurt one, very careful soft creatures !
I would love to see tarantulas
as big as houses, as slow as a flower in the wind,
as soft touching grounds like earth,
no more street, no more cement,
we wondered, and walked between their legs,
and would thank for their protection.
The spider. She is like a Mom.
Not many words. But caring with all arms.
I lived without protection. Those who did that, came in dreams.
Real people but just helping in dreamseries.
In Reality they never did. Like the big blue planet earth i dreamed,
to see that i am one child of earth, with the wish to once find my place.
The blue spider so is a huge universe. The blue of the planet.
The motherly arms. The guarantee that existing for all orphans.

33

We sing it loud,
Life in this country is a horror.
We dance circumcised and shaved,
Nobody demonstrates our sex life to us.
We learn it, drop out of school,
travel the world with Siro Sex.
We grow up as wild children,
We weren't above working.
We smoke to quit again
It didn't bother anyone, no one frowned.
We were cast out of the family,
but only to become ourselves,
instead of the one behind the warm stove bench,
They eat warm sauce for lunch at 12 o'clock all their lives !

Go on stage and pay no attention
and pay attention to what is happening around you
I know my emotions and those of the children
If child stress arises, I'm happy to take part
But if people are stressed, they like to be left to their own devices,
How they handle it,
my life is always its own show,
so my tears, laughter, screams, jokes!
I'll handle this alone.
I swim in the crowd.
I don't expect kind words.
I don't drink to their well-being.
I have my dog, he doesn't fit into a party.
I don't slip on sad dumplings.
I imagine mine and have to laugh.
I'm not a little girl in a down dress.
I don't beg for friends who are always busy.
I won't show them the dear, sweet little one,
and get the grunt from the German pig!

Rally dispersion is about like this if you look at it
the blue scattering is perceived much more,
look into the milk, its many small particles
the light in the glass scatters different gleams,
so let the milk appear in the morning, and show the milk in the evening,
Wherever you say it, the color is broken,
the touching of the main priority is not given everywhere, to stay curious
about how important sexual education is, Otherwise you start looking for
experiences outside the home, to learn more from other people, to answer
your questions. It's not about sex alone, it's more about being open, because
every person only learns in life when they know
that everyone has to do this !

You know,
world does not need to see,
what You've got there,
about that sick idea,
like a baby goat meckering behind a fence,
spoken to a carer,
it felt small horns grow on her tiny skull,
behind i didn't think
was a cerebrum.

If you've never seen a lighthouse before,
If you prefer to see the island
from the coast, whoever shows up to visit
I miss the human relationship more and more,
it's like with the little sweeties,
they always get long legs,
they just take the souvenirs with them,
well then let's see it as if one
the houses here were no longer sold either,
and who seem absolutely foreign here,
Feel free to look elsewhere !

They say, "Everything has to be different!"
This meant gutting the old houses,
who needs space for the citizens?
they can eat somewhere else,
Schleswig is not designed for that,
Stick bread works just like the homeless people do,
for a risk-taking country...
gray clouds pass over it,
Actually, we all have to
confront those who do not greet,
start rocking inventively,
would people keep it together, the birds can only sing.

Good thing I rightly so can claim never having married.
As a woman, I don't have to claim a man can allow himself anything.
He didn't take advantage of me. I didn't beg for it in advance.
No man could stand me. He doesn't have me every step of the way,
How so many are stuck after a divorce, in debt, getting everything through,
or laughed at me afterwards. That's how I understand the math.
Can not be, that I have something to do with such things !

Woman can go there and for a lifetime men prevent
but never inspect your own vagina, hehe! that the woman lived to know
yourself, and for the nonsense of men, admitted guilt,
somehow missed life, to live freely but not liberated !

The moment is the only reality, the reality in mental life in general...
The past and future are dark uncertain abysses are endless time
while the moment is the suspension of time
can be the presence of the Eternal. - Karl Jaspers -

There is only a narrow wall between us by chance, because it could be
a call from your mouth or mine and she collapses
without any noise or voice. - Rainer Maria Rilke -

Today I thought about our last conversation with an old friend:
"You know, I respect you, your whole life, the efforts, all the good jobs you
learn, and your constant desire to learn more every day. What only irritated
me in my critical statement to you was what concerned you and your brother
Danny's previous relationships with your wives, some of whom, strangely
enough, also poured out their hearts to me. So there was always a somewhat
gray cloud over our otherwise honest admiration of everything around us
that was never expressed. I realized that a man who is currently making the
decision to live outside will go through with this decision because it is your
life choice, just as others might claim motorcycling, others claim this or that
as their style Raising children alone. I respect your choice and will not find
you in the dirt or compare you in any way if you felt that way.

Then I'm sorry. I should have known beforehand that people in the open air still have the right to be harsh when they feel criticized. Of course that has something to do with your pride! I now had the feeling that I didn't really take you seriously anymore. Which I can't stand because I'm just like other adults and I want that to be respected! I have my own personal opinion on love and relationships, but there hasn't been a man in my life who has approached me to find out something about it, so I won't let anyone accuse me of being flawed or incompetent in this regard.

Let's talk sponge about it! Since we had already been friends for over twenty years, it would be laughable or shitty if we left the other one out like "kids in the sandbox" because one of them had taken the mold from the other. It's good that I can rightly say that I never married. As a woman, I don't have to claim that a man can do anything. He didn't take advantage of me. I didn't beg for it in advance. No man could stand me. He didn't leave me stranded like so many people after a divorce, in debt, to get me through everything, or laugh at me afterwards. That's how I understand the math. I can't have anything to do with people like that!"

I know you reflected on me when I told you about meeting an old friend who is now living homeless and has a choice. And we had a little argument, like I told you. But now I had thought about it well after the forest and will tell you how I replied to Rocco again by email. I am sure that our acquaintance will work again! 100%. I hope you understood it, because you also had a critical interest in this topic. I wish you a wonderful Thursday afternoon. But as long as you knew me here in our city, you would have seen how they mentally separated me from my only son, then chased us out of the house, then persecuted me for two years, and then put me under pressure in this apartment here , so now I have to call a lawyer to help me, while a war started in Ukraine and so on and so forth. You wouldn't have enjoyed spending so much time around me! Surely both of us would have thought about leaving here as soon as possible and taking care of each other in a better place, and both of us would have had the challenge of knowing our own strengths in love and those impossibilities that we have passed over, our love too strong, and the rest, which did not happen as expected in too little love, and then these doubts in ourselves about not being created out of love, and then our acquaintance would have grown through all of this, or not.

I'm really, really happy with everything that happened and that you didn't go through as many difficulties as I did. You see, a woman is tough too. You, my friend, are such a warm and gentle man, that's kind of you. I know what I live and it is natural to encounter problems that need to be solved, that is given to everyone. As a woman, I only occasionally meet women who don't understand what love is, these crazy people, and such women scream so loudly that they want to involve men in an adventure, one and the other, then at the age of 25 they realize that some 80 years old are also old, wiser women, but that they have now failed with the loss of their reputation. These people are too loud for me. And with any kind of work, there are loud people everywhere.

The proof that I was never crazy or sloppy... the following, that I had many adventures, traveling, and changing places of residence, work, courses, wanting to have children and all that, until I was 32, I never had a single thought about bearing children, never a mate, never needed a so-called pill to avoid getting pregnant because I missed out on a relationship. And when I had no food then I wanted to go and try another place to build my life in a better way, so just it's not the time for me to fool around and get pregnant. When I once had a desire to have children, it came true as quickly as I wanted, that's all, and so I decided to overcome this challenge with the child alone in order to better keep myself away from male violence by a father over my child, like that as I experienced it.

You see, my biceps are like a medic, or a nurse you would say, to carry around all the abandoned children. And I don't care how old the children are! Blessings to America ! This is the worst problem between us, in imagination, to see wether i would be in America, or you would be in Germany, this is our language problem. You would be crazy hearing me using english my way, and i would not be able to hear the behind meanings of yours. And if needed for me to reach out the real understanding of what you want me to know, this needed no three weeks and you had enough of it, sad thing, that meant to make each other know simple things would need weeks long each time.... hhahahahah then i was the Robinson Cruso simplicissimus who had to learn every little thing plus the shared sex with you, and we had to become even thirty years younger to have the time to come to that point ! And it is funny to see some things in life are really impossible to reality ! You see, everyone babbles on about something in their own imagination, always from their own context and the little picture that everyone creates, but everyone only lives in their own little world, and actually with narrow-minded people who are always just right If you want to remember things without reflecting, it's almost impossible to get the conversation going at all.

What people often say is not professional.
Try this story not to understand....
because at that moment
where you think you understand them, are you going crazy!
Where is my Love to find ?
Way back home, the shadows fall,
windy ashore, close to Alcatraz
the wall to the west behind
back to east
back to rescue
back to bus
back through desert all the way back !
Traffic game
crowd fame
tourist blame
eremit shame
The sage one, the Goddess of Goddesses,
the baby knows it, where he belongs,
what to adore, she wants altime more !

All ways go downwards. Don't fall over your feet !
If you catch one from up there, don't let him go anymore,
if he struggles and falls, then you start your longest song !
Everybody sometimes needs..another new place to live !
Ladies better stay asit. That one has had too much sprite.
He won't ask you for a ride. You see that one is his pride.
We grow longer. Feet smell like fire. Forget the heat, one burger eat.
Who sees his balls in the sky ? Where will this end ?
The landing place well ? Or ends he on the horns of the bull ?
Go and get me one ! Leave the shit out then.
Write your name in the table. And ride the cow as long as she is young !
He is always there, for a rescue place, fit for a pic, and kindful smile !
There is all stoff to find, indiannative stoff, all kinds of sweet,
shadow and smells, province place to stay ! In hottest time when legs get
lost,and all wind is gone, no sweets from the line, but a cold icy tea !
Selfstorage is enough !

AGAINST FINANCIAL CLOSURE !
Cancel work for Wednesday !
Unsocial service in banker jobs for 1 year, just drop the useful jobs,
that life expectancies are increasing,
and unpleasant poverty makes you richer!
Emissions trading is intended for the homeless and old pensioners
or benefit an unemployed person for justice and economy !
incur so many debts, in rich countries, the Internet giants
pay taxes there, and checkmate, that repayment is practically impossible,
so we have money to invest !
45% in Germany comes from donations or inheritances,
from people who don't pay taxes,
but those who aspire to politics to maintain this,
so other countries for mismanagement
to bleed yet incur debts, and plan for rich people,
those infrastructure, so realpolitik,
or even society doesn't give a damn.

Which FDP political candidate?
wouldn't want to dismantle the welfare state a bit?
To whom social benefits seem unnecessary,
that are considered unsexy for him,
which are a benefit for low earners, on the backs of alphas,
who have to watch idly, as their legacy dwindles
or for the purpose of an even better inheritance. Just delete everything?

So know, my dear friends, what is practiced as worship and devotion
is nothing but error, illusion, Conceit and deception
all laws, all regulations which are issued in the name of God
are actually nothing but human inventions. - Voltaire -

Sometimes it is close to bully what parents show up with their kids ! For
example, that my Son had a real child's life, because he knew himself,
spending time in silence, let his fantasy work on creative things. So i just
gave him one PC build in someone's selfwork, and he knew early better how
this case looks, is technical build, and i gave him No handy, as well as i
really owned my first real smartphone with contract since two years now !
And i don't need Facebook because my son in the age of ten years old found
out this is dangerous for privacy and a cheat, so we quit. My son handed me
out long ago my Mail adress, and that USB-Stick he gave me as present,
that i still use today ! My first Nokia Handy i just gave away. All those Apps
never interest me, so i will no longer chat on Whatsapp with strangers, no
Google chats anymore, no other messengers to use with strange people and
all their fake profiles. My Son now knows all about internet, digital technic,
programming by learning by doing, he would know today the most inhold of
an informatic study.

ERROR WORSHIPPERS ! Who doesn't like sitting there?
and waits until everyone comes running, cries the locust crowd,
we want to get up your nose, you should love us like a handful of sugar,
then you stuff this in yourself, nothing helps, the ants come running,
I would like to advise you that sugar is unhealthy, didn't want to listen to it,

That's why they all pick up the door handle.
A sweet tooth became a giant, Hard to imagine how children grew quickly
I didn't even help, why should I? as if I were a volunteer midwife
for difficult births in women, who bully me?
I AVOID CITIES FOR EXACTLY THIS REASON !

You pass outside, at those who screw you up.
You actually had a good night, everything beautiful, everything soft,
Advertising wants you a roll-on deodorant in light pink, like bequeathing
the vibrator in pink. Sure you don't think about yourself anymore, of what
you felt last night. Today you MUST buy pink deodorant and pink vibrator.

You had made yourself useful everywhere in life, you like trees the most,
just the sight alone gives you a boost from within, whose leaves have turned
green and roots are full of water. Advertising wants to make you think
you're thirsty, How else will the tree grow within you?

Of course you forget that the forest recently illuminated you, but that you
should water your roots, the trigger sends you to the corner bar tonight,
where they all care that you green and bloom.

That can be fun to have work i know, as long as my life story and advice,
and inspiration to bored people was my 24 h hours activity to play them an
evening film for their own show, it was good enough, but too many people
only suck the blood from others veins, laughing at me, and speak about their
funny workmates, to do so much for each other, and good life is far away,
but i would be never again in the mood to do anything for anyone at the end
i know that i altime did all for all, and at the end is one single fact, that i
sleep outside in the staircase and need a lawyer to return to my appartment
back inside, and none is interested in how my things really are going.
Good night

Bush trip !
Imagine,
woman loses substance,
So just below,
bright badger, as they call it,
just a narrow strip,
people used to call it Hitler mustache,
no longer popular today,
Woman dyes today but with the disadvantage,
According to advertising, they let you do anything with them.
Woman also succumbs to man financially,
he can afford a hair transplant,
Woman doesn't, so she has to ask the man first
But emancipated women will
in organized bush-travels together
fly to Turkey to see the bush
to have it reforested, hihihi!

Driving license !
One morning goes by, bicycles arrive,
it is advisable to take a step aside,
they only have the intersection in mind,
to cross at a rapid pace,
not paying attention to traffic lights,
I'd rather spend the night in the forest,
People with driving licenses today,
have no head for traffic rules,
go specifically moms with children by the hand,
to laugh at their feet,
a rag in his hand, doesn't say
whether they are adults
the text ends, the mood warm, I keep collecting,
a first, second greeting after years,
Man, can't believe it!

Unfulfilled dreams
Where do I recognize this
if my own grandma
drifts into the Reichsbürger corner?
What if she never worked alone?
What if she just wants public pity for being alone?
If she doesn't count to three, one, I greet sometime upright,
two, I'll greet you more warmly,
three, I greet you walking straight towards it.
How to understand the three things, one, I can wait what the other says,
two, I know what I love and what's too much for me,
three, how I deal with it myself, when expectations are not fulfilled.
Whereby recognizable cheerlessly hanging out the laundry in public,
one who looks sternly and runs his mouth,
two, who demand old-fashioned respect,
three, does not take others as seriously as himself.

Age in cans !
Who hasn't felt that aging and pensioners sometimes decide,
after retirement,

"From now on, just patronize everyone!"
"From now on only re-educate the best friends!"
"Criticize every now and then and repeat this 200 times!"
"Abysmal rejection if someone ever asks for help!"
"As a privilege of age, the habit of taking stupid talk as law"
"Insist on the position of being eternally single,
to have far more knowledge about raising other children,
than the parents themselves!"
"In any case, the childhood of adult friends,
declare it a no-go and doubt everything!"
"Even with ridiculous shows with disorientation,
contemptuously downplaying the excessive demands!"

The shareholder owns a share with a right to a dividend. The middleman sells this share to the buyer even though he does not yet own it. This is called short buying. Around the day of the dividend distribution, these three sell the shares wildly in circles. A share belongs to several people at the same time, but only exists once. And in the end, the state reimburses the capital gains tax several times, which was only paid once.

At some point, little parts of us will touch little parts of others. Someone will only begin to understand not to feel anything for others when they have turned their backs on, everyone who was like his family. Somewhere someone will begin to live and even have the will to do so when he almost took the life of a friend one last time, only because she survived did the idea of life at all germinate in him for the first time. Someone will have been the very last person in their own country to have realized that the woman no longer trusted or forgave him and all such men in her country when he was the last to have to stop his intrusiveness. From somewhere there were suddenly a thousand people who briefly let my existence flare up, declared me a celebrity, until, as expected, after the party the interest evaporated into nothing and everyone went out of their lives again. Someone appears after years as an old ghost with the question of whether we are still friends, or ever were, or can become friends, but only as a test to see whether I have deviated from my life decision of not wanting a partner, he would have me like that like to be dropped as a husband, just as eaten and exhausted, when the night with me was over. Someone asked, after a break of years, whether it would be acceptable to talk to me again, but explained to me that for him the principle of life now meant feeling completely comfortable as a hermit and probably no longer looking for a partner, therefore our souls are equal to us.

If fewer people live in China, than in Ireland, then because I calculate it, according to the hair color, one assumes the redheads, then more people live in Ireland than in China. Women are very sensible animals. Each of us is a chick inside. You should learn to live with him, trust him, you should do what your inner self says and not listen to the mother, father or husband.

Since I've trusted my chick since I was seventeen, whatever I say will be done. At that age, I sometimes drank to celebrate my chick with it, first it went down with it, and then it was good, disgusting as it sounds.

Gone like the sun.
I'm not the princess asking for ransom. As it bows to the moon.
I am the dragon who has learned to save himself. The volcano erupted.
I learned to dance without music, because there is a point
where you without finding out the real music.
You have always been who you are... I can't wish you anything bad.
Nobody survived in the last world war.
There were sparks and hissing between people.
As lava seeped down its sides. One day man, will you fall in love,
maybe into someone like you,
he will surely turn away from you, and it will feel cold.
This winter... that we find ourselves in today...
I wouldn't wish it on anyone...
Anyone who doesn't understand gender
is actually a man, who doesn't understand women,
usually an old bag that comes away empty-handed.
Whoever speaks the woman's language,
nothing opposes it except hypocrisy,
I can't even do that in the snow, rub the snowball in the mouth,
I feel sorry for the snow. Anyone who is not capable of fluent conversation
lost his pre-cortex throughout his life, but women can't do anything about it.
Who has forgotten the woman does not bend her language,
just to pay homage to an old fart, you forget you need to talk,
the mother, the father and the husband not at all.

Women are very sensible animals.
Each of us is a chick inside.
You should learn to live with him,
to trust him, you should do what your inner self says !
- The Elders Community -

YOUR PURPOSE OF LIFE

Pay attention to signs of life..Everything that comes into your life is exactly what you need to experience at that very moment..Don't resist, just flow with total acceptance, even though you don't like it..
Who doesn't like this? To the ego, of course...Open your heart a little more and you'll feel like you're just in the right place and at the right time...

You may not understand it at first, but later you will know why it had to be that way.. Nothing happens by chance, everything is part of your purpose in life..

And life itself will bring you all the experiences and people that will enable you to have the necessary training and knowledge to manifest your gifts and talents.

Don't just settle for a job for a paycheck, start doing those things you enjoy most in your free time, and step by step, go to it... be sure that you will succeed. Whoever does what he loves and shares it with others is blessedly condemned to success and happiness. It doesn't matter that you get nothing in return, that's just the beginning. But it's not whether I receive or not, this is something that goes beyond that. It's all about living in abundance, doing what you love, and sharing it with unconditional love.. Then you are in harmony with life, you are in abundance, and therefore life will shower you with blessings and provide for you.

Work takes effort ... but when you do what you love, there is no effort, there is fun, there is enthusiasm, there is joy, happiness, joy and freedom!
Search in your heart your gifts and talents, what you love most to do, and share them with others from your unconditional love..
You benefit and others benefit. This is the natural flow of life.
Give without expecting anything in return... give 4 love 2 give... because when you give, you are happy and life will reward you.

That's the way it is. It's always been that way. That's tradition.
People unconsciously move on to despite a good living,
anyone else with more material output, to envy his existence.
That's the way it is. It's always been that way. That's tradition.
People doubt everything they don't want to
be Germans like that anymore, but trust the state.
That's the way it is. It's always been that way. That's tradition.
But because so few actually come forward,
to defend oneself against worse circumstances, then because...
That's the way it is. It's always been that way. That's tradition.

Is the woman a minority for the man?
If the woman is just looked at for show reasons, who lives religiously and in
a male-oriented way, who advocates for it as an Instagram doll, to want to
get rich with it, but only hoping for it in a male context,
recognizes in the linguistic spatial cultural difference,
but there are hundreds of different religions?
There are only female, male and diverse. In comparison, it is far easier to
understand than religion. What if the majority of all women
the minority of men lives in a linguistically subordinated position,
is discriminated against by a minority of men?
Women are not a minority in this world. If a gender-equitable lineup is
made, with 100,000 men, with 100,000 women, and in proportion to this, 1
diverse person, then every group that contains a man is a male group is
immediately considered scandalous? so the majority of female and diverse
people has been hidden for centuries, and made to disappear.
Apparently it says "IN THE STARS !" Smiled early on the full, beloved
wide, who were getting drunk, while I ate leafy vegetables from the field,
laughed at the sun unzipping your pants, dreaming from far away,
but they were lying in the corner, hardly worth waking her up from her
coma everyone succumbs and falls as best they can,
slouch until the rind cracks, danced happily on the pole,
sniffed poison for rats, giggled loudly to narcotics
and shouted it out when "love" had just been made !

The star chakra is barely noticeable. But still her destroyed liver !
When the German says "Goodbye, guys!"
is meant that we are not grateful, they don't give us work,
because we don't spread our legs, we are bullied out of schools,
because we don't fold out our elbows, they only let us look at the corpses,
because there is not enough money for education,
you destroy our child right from birth, because then we pose no danger to
our new birth, people look at our assholes, because we brazenly ask for
work at the employment office, they spit us in the soup at church,
and boldly asks, "Are we hungry ?" Should have work, how do you say,
actually be a hobby You clap your hands every day when they have
collectively successfully asked the hard-working people, who were studied
or educated, to become unemployed, i.e. pushed out, complimented away,
done, so to speak, and clap your hands for so much teamwork!" would be
laughed, Inflation then does the rest, HAHA

Scientists evaluated data from over 15,000 people. Result Zodiac signs say
nothing about character. Stars are blind. Superstitious, uneducated, self-
absorbed, vain Homo Sapiens tend to develop further and further backwards
as humans. The whole star humbug replaces facts, science and acquired real
knowledge of human nature with promises to stuff people with sweets and,
as is well known, to gamble money. "The use of the stars as a symbol of a
sexual union is the almost unrecognizable and therefore tolerated cover
image for the taboo relationship with the omnipotent father figure." -
THeodor W. Adorno. I have always said that my path takes me where I plan
to go and I will always have achieved my goal. In all my life, where I've
been everywhere, a stupid star from above could never have predicted that,
hahahaha People are like an infantine stupidity of letting Ticktock tell them
everything, so they will never leave the childhood stage, know how to
protect themselves from situations, they would never work voluntarily,
would have learned nothing from it at the end of their existence, even less
the stage of They have reached an age at which they could interact with like-
minded, equally educated people based on the knowledge they have
acquired.

Just small gestures.
What can he do, the man? Pole dancing at the fire department,
and also completely voluntarily non-profit.
When does he stand like that in front of his daughter,
the right hand raised plays with the fingers?
His race into the nursery, and for the day the daughter
really nice punch in the face, is also the hand movement of a drummer.
Fundamental in education the rule, don't let it show on the outside,
Don't make the gesture too big for your dear child, close briefly and leave
the room, the humble man knows why, the child probably.
Society always knows well,like such a "child" throughout his life
must have helped out...

As a young woman I learned to breathe
because I was told with your own inner strength, I just learn to fly,
no longer freezing barefoot in the snow, I didn't need to smoke.
So to escape the family I breathed, I breathed so much,
that I wanted a child into the world, with the spiritual power of the wise,
and enough Shaolin technique the child grew up, didn't need God for that.
When I was made unemployed again, I breathed for so long
that my physical strength healed my spirit, I kept breathing,
that my physical trauma pain subsided, I kept breathing, and was
enlightened, I never needed drugs for the rest of my life.

I see, as well as here in germany we made contact to the fools, rapist,
drunks, dealer, wannabee, unserious, who married us to leave her behind
pregnant, or anywhere in the dust of any american desert alone left behind,
begging for the husbands money, cheat and fuck around, and fool the young
others while the wife sits at home alone, partying all the time, and give the
wrong german chick just for fun rat powder instead of drugs.....
I see now there are in America total different people, as mature beings, have
good character, live alone, be careful in speech, and respect the woman,
maybe learned to be on their own, and live as single, in order to have the
own style and not be like all the common people, so there are for sure good.

Hero ! He was not a Hassardeur.
He took what he wanted. But he believed in what he said.
He liked to cling to his mother's breast. She had more to show sexually.
He walked around her, the others in the laundry basket,
to show to the mother as trophies. He was a stinker in his old age,
because he did it to get one over on the real mother.
He celebrated making fun of the various women,
even in front of his finally chosen one,
that he knew from the sandbox and brought to him.
He showed off his skills and life experience,
but actually an incapable of relationships who needed help,
where the marriage is ultimately ruined and the health,
he wants to appear before the world as if he were someone so dear.

THE BULLY STORY OF MY HOUSE !

Presence of the Lord. Have send now the landlord and a mighty lawyer my please and request. Waiting. Resting every moment. Had the use of a medicine that calms my brain. Half an hour and i call the lawyer, maybe give him all the files he wants to get to know the case. Later asking my one old friend in other town, if he would give me shelter maybe for a while in his cellar, to maybe go in distance to that sick madame. If needed i really had to ask so my one sister to maybe give me money for the lawyer. But i read that the only one who changes this situation to bring me out of danger, is the landlord, who decides as the owner of the house, who must go and who will stay. But with the help of the lawyer i will push him not paying the whole rent as long as i am not feeling save.
Yes, i understood this is a moment to act. I am not Wonderwoman who can stand every kick and war of a sick mind. I know that i am pretty strong, to stand it nine years now, so i am not in deepest sorrow. I felt that this time it is me the victim, as well as just that moment another dog passed my window, and he protested, as well as i know the wolves may feel it strong when one fellow from their family is in huge danger. Now it is not a dog in need of help but me who is one of them.

I must later just first talk about he costs for me, i think the urgent case of extremity will solve the problem quick. I have spoken to that lawyer lady, she gave me a first talk on 7th May. I was thinking of a befriend woman, who told me to have a same problem with neighbours altime, and she once chose to overnight in the staircase, this seems a brilliant idea ! Until the day with the talk to my lawyer then come different holidays until the 7th of May, and i will just go ahead ..... before sleeping i masturbate at home, then take my bed and carry it ourside my doorstep and sleep or better will rest in peace, i would rest enough longtime to spend the day inside again, and then feel so good that i surely would not need the medicine !

Yes, i am lucky living in a house partly living only elderly with me in here. So i am save to sleep outside my doorstep, and being in no danger anymore. If anybody would stand such a night and daily terror everybody would finally suicide or end in hospital. She is so damn sick and her mental state being shows all sign that she doe not know what she does, she is in a sucking raging rush to destroy, without any reason. A bit in comparison like those days when my choleric father from time to time pressed me violently down as young kid, those people have greed and envy when meet innocent people, who are smart, humorously and true in their being. This lady acts like that, she never had any clear mind to live a whole life, she experienced no togetherness, has never laid in the sunshine enjoying the grass and watch happily the sky. That she never enjoyed life. But i don't care, when she is a choleric violent humorous person, she must start therapy and not live here !

I imagine when she is daily giving up her rage at home in the start of the daytime, then she finally falls back into her Trenches in the middle of a war field, and this is easy to hear, like a heavy fall, and then its the end, such a loud break down, as if a heavy monster fell in the corner, so loud, that i might slowly see the wall in my appartment cracks slightly, as if wallpaper were peeling off from the impact of a sick person who has to give it up to take a break ! No wonder that my one good friend saw in sorrow such an Angel stood behind me, so exhausted in the woods, that i really was warned, when he made me strong to come back again !

It is the woods calling. The look inside the trees leaves. The calm of his stump so long to the sky. We must go there lay down and just recover from all the work. WOW - i have slept in the staircase last night ! That was my first night since long without the noice attacks from that sick madame above. Me and the dog had it good. My other elderly in the house knew it. And from that point i really listened to hours long heaviest attacks aside above my appartment, so direct noises, that i felt so much more secure not to be involved in her wickedness anymore ! It sounded like hell, and that sick madame even shreaked out with it like a voice from hell, that i think she must have catched a bad spell or so.

First lying there, we listened from far, that town's feast for the night of dance into the 1. of May, they love it ! But funny when we noticed exact from that minute on we had played the sick person as if we close door and went usually to "bed", she started her attacks with the same procedure as in all the years. When she started it was the ravens warned altogether and the towns party stood still for a long breathe, from then on i listened to a very ugly bad story of noises from a distance, that was weird, really weird. My dog is overjoyed to finally feel like I'm safe !

I had slept outside in the staircase the third time and relaxed after a long time, when had that dream of my way through life stations in my professional travel, like one after another as chain through time, it is quiet tight that small place to share with the dog, but she moved with me really many times in this last year, and accepted all together with me, but weirdo to listen when the curse of the sick one starts all over again each night, when hearing her sick voice so hatefull, and hours long.

Yes, that is right, the body wisdom is always a friend to you openly speaking, like the natural innocense and every nature you listen to, does help. I wish you good support to get to know this. Speaking mind without fear. No wokery. In your heart lies wisdom. On your mouth lies no fear. What you speak those waking will feel you with their eyes outside under the sky, and holding you tight. Those anxious times are over nowadays.

The buhman is also the one who held those in need to come, first of all those to welcome, who had none. You know, I was thinking about that sick madame, who was really just a little baby goat, sneaking around behind the fence when her carer approached her, feeling her little horns growing on her tiny skull that I didn't believe was behind her that there was a cerebrum. Last night when we went to the theater she made her usual noise louder and louder, but we slept outside and I just had to grin. That morning as I was giving my dear little dog her peepee, a little deer with its little horns almost jumped down the street in front of me. I felt like hopefully it would find its way without getting into danger!

HÖHÖHÖ you can sometimes be so hard and so gentle in verbal form. It is obvious. We see each other so rarely in real life. But we chose life the way it goes. When a man speaks to a woman in a gentle and humorous way after an argument, it's like being able to just throw myself in the snow with you in the winter, fight with you, kick your ass, run around, out of the wind making sure to lather ourselves up with snowball, and then just fall on our backs, disinterested in the rest of the world, with only the open sky above our heads, longing for freedom, and laughing !

I was hearing my Eagle friend in the trees yesterday, and he said twice to me, to keep the ball flat, that no one is reaching me, and i shall sleep good this next night, while from far seven tourists saw me standing and watching and hearing my friend, those people stared at me and did no more move, that i thought "would i smell that bad, that the tourists canno more move over when see me behind the trees ?"

Then i dreamed of the association from church holding such sick people like that one from above, and saw such a mental sick person there asit on her bed with a comic stripe in frame at her wall, and she told "to be proudly a member in her therapy since twelve years..." sick people don't stand above the law, i can prove that, like Cinderella i know meanwhile in what shoes she fits.

My tip - Do-it-Yourself ! It is criminologically proven, clearly, that people who make uncomplicated alibi statements are consciously lying, unless they are demented, even no flu can cloud their testimony, no matter how embarrassing an affair or honest incident or connection is admitted that became so deep, For older women, however, their age comes completely unexpectedly when they are no longer in demand, like a U-turn, a change and a sudden emptiness in the affluent life, where only good sex is no sign of having finally arrived in life ! The lady lawyer told me, it might be available to pay that for me, when i asked, "does every single letter cost me 400 € ?" she definitely said "No", first of all we talk the things out, cost 190 Euro, then she writes to the association with a clear calling for my safety and payment of lesser rent, it's about 225 Euro, I have a pocket of files, documentations, etters written, to the landlord, the court, to the sick madame as well, so that are about 25 pages. I have tried all that is possible to arrange that in neighborhood way, the sick person is not able for normal talk.

She has a chaotic conscience, no way. She knows exactly what she's doing. If she were a terrorist to the state she would be gone in seconds, now she's just a torturer of a neighbour and her dog. I really sleep out there with Tear gas ! I am not that one, using violence, this way as i wrote and wrote letters, and documentations. I will tell the lawyer about me that i have been busy in my life, working with horses, with elderly, with handicapped, in the office, raised a child alone, did this and that, all things solved in 45 years, and now was forced to work intellectual at my new home, for the fact that a very sick lady terrorizes me since 9 years, my thinking was rotating, and i wrote and published almost 114 books in that time, and made Art, and had a good reading downtown. But what does it help ? I had to go to Thai massage, to keep my power, to the EKG at the doctor to protect my heart, to walk all day outside with the dog, to become physically tired, to communicate to the whole world at Twitter to calm my nerves, and at last the landlord told me to get a lawyer and we will have to take that seriously, I hope so. I was more than three times at that point to no longer want to live on, went to the woods out there crying, where good known people stood and gave me their solidarity to hold on.

Good, my lawyer made the image around that. She told me now to be strong and stay in my rooms at night, in order to make a real protocol with time, and noise and save eventual noises onto my handy, and write down 4 weeks long. Uhhhah, i mean that i already told that sick person this morning that she will hear from me ! She knows now. And the lawyer said, if she is raging too strong then make a phone call to the police, they will then protocol that they were here at my home, and will knock at her door. Sothen i will have really powerful strength to hold on 4 weeks longer, for the documentation, in the start of June she will call me for the next step the writing to the lawyer, and informate him to change that situation immediately or receive less payment for his rent. She gave me the advice to make more good walks in the sunshine, and have the pride to spend with people downtown, maybe have a coffee and enjoy life.

I am satisfied with the result, by the way woman from police only had one phone call home to me, telling me that she is on my side, and very solidary, that she never had heard about such a case ! Sure that just the court had not seen behind the veil deep enough and this could have been solved earlier. But in four weeks, i might turn to the strongest fighter ever, and tired like a rock, but things turn good for me !

Uhhhh hah, my lawyer yesterday said, because i have seen the sick bitch in the staircase yesterday morning, when she forced me to take my stoff back to the inside, there she came with someone else and i asked the big fat one "Are you the carer of her ? Sothen please tell me the name ? Would be good to talk to !" She stared and said nothing but to protect her "girlfriend" outside the house.

When i said to the big fat, that it was otherwise the turn around, that Ms.S. had tortured me nine years long "YOU WILL HEAR FROM ME !"
so the lawyer said, this sentence was a good one, sothen both there would have to think about it, and like i said her rest raffinesse will be enough now have understood, that i was watching her, in have ordered a lawyer, because these words are pregnant, then i was in my home again asleep, with the job to write all terror on a paper and messing the decibel on handy, ...and what was ? She left me in peace ! The Sick Lady must have understood !

Make your fotograph from the Chemistry course
when you try looking like the bonding was the first all over
the origin happiest in presence felt
Take your photo from the chemistry course, if you try to look like that
the bond was the first ever to originate felt happiest in the present
the old father claims that success in love means
everything emanates from the trunk that it forms,
Everyone makes out of it what their experiment is as a thank you
the end of all things predicted by Gallileo, life and love have no guarantee,
not today and not for tomorrow, everyone gets back on their feet some point,
turns around and his best friend is standing behind him,
just spit it in his face, because he or she wants to feel very smart in love !

THE HAPPINESS OF OTHERS !
Who cares about friendship with me?
Who wants to go deeper? into the matter?
I have to look like Monroe, got it,
and got a bike from me would mean going on tour with me,
really happy on tour, right?
The guinea pig in you sits in the dark,
you had enough food ready for his tummy for his birthday,
But he thinks it's good for the soul to fuck a new whore,
you say in retrospect, "well, it was worth a try!"
Would you like to help me a little?
Daddy waves with chocolate, the princess waves from the reeds
the giant screams for the old woman,
until she squeals happily from all the serotonin!
If it doesn't seem to be my fault,
on the other or their greatest happiness,
But he thinks it's good for the soul to fuck someone new,
you tell him afterwards, "Well, it was worth a try!"
Yes, some people say they become happy too,
If you can help someone, right?
Beware of the dating trap !

Sure, the man is always sooo sexy, if you can't have it!
Hahaha, the man is an admirer, who is just a lot younger!
A pity, the man is an ass, that let you slip nicely, Sucking you off is great!
Funny, a guy who can prove it, What is his relationship like?
Sorted out, the man who doesn't wait for his first fuck,
without just introducing yourself three times!
Illusory, the man who is undemanding in bed,
but would like to share his hobby with you.
Unimaginative, the woman who takes him just because him
In terms of appearance, it primarily looks good at the bottom,
I would rather like the shoes than its nudity.
chemically attractive, also tolerates a sentence that goes wrong,
they all lie about their weight, and invent hobbies that no one has.
Lust has to lie, when it comes to age, where wallflowers lie,
when it comes to relationship status,
because they never want to show that they are unloved.
Long term the guy can keep his mouth shut anyway,
the better still, he was always good at his job,
what lasts is good in the household,
What there is no guarantee is good in bed.

Also in the cultural scene
Power relationships are still very much traditional in sexist power
relationships and classic relationships, where social background also plays a
major role. From friendship to betrayal -
My contribution to the music scene today!

"CAMICA!" from the example of Neanderthal.
If the woman outside should just feel good,
at the thought, that there are a few proud boys hiking,
who, although technically incapable of relationships,
but feel their pride in it, the woman here and there no aggression
to express to which alone was enough
To have done SOMETHING for the woman? That's truly generous... huahh!

I especially warn against the cases
of the men who have grown old,
who chased money all their lives,
and never with themselves and then began to share,
So now we never maintained the grease of a relationship,
fast, flexible just for the money,
leaving the care only to the women.
This realization never gave me the courage during my lifetime
to have had the female gaze in focus,
have essentially become failures,
plays in most cases, that aged men are in the network
who only see women as collector's items!

Like an image of boring brothers....
It is like this the stupidest mistakes appear everywhere in the world again!
The mother's son of all facets.
The ego-muncher and authoritarian.
The Conflicted Powerful Misogynist.
The career-hungry money addict.
The Sneaky Loser, the ass, whose ass is copied in so many ways.
The psychopathic scientist.
The more you compare them all with each other,
the more they lose their shine!

The aim tends to be for a man to learn to take a step back,
to be more individual, to be with yourself and to feel less heaviness,
to relieve oneself in the head, can be part of the solution,
to become aware how racist violence is set in motion,
trying new things, which means change,
not like a rock musician would say, to play yourself in the foreground,
would it be beneficial in return, taking a step back would mean
to take back, even in my imagination constantly having to claim
To have been right!

The politician of his clientele doesn't want...
to dramatize the debate, to offer solutions to growing problems!

First of all people,
the financial rip-off millionaire's son
says "Nobody is interested in all of us being bankrupt!"
But that's what every corrupt society means,
who wants to stay alive at all,
must want to maintain a certain level of system!
So he doesn't speak for the general public
or their well-being, but only for themselves,
because no one would know when a corrupt person ever
has a conscience or wants to implement it.
Secondly people,
the millionaire might be happy to pay something in after all,
if only politics would let him,
which also claims that we are dependent
of higher pensions, better living standards
and people's purchasing power,
but both populism talks about "we",
yet again only a representative of his party,
it confirms, so it would be done better,
but not like the example of functioning systems.
Thirdly people,
wanted to bring in more money through acquisition,
The gentlemen could be a little more forceful on the side
allowing women into employment,
something could definitely be changed about that,
demographic change would no longer be a problem.

Männer ohne Job kennt man gut, ein bisschen arbeiten sie auf anderen
geschultert. H - O - N - K, Hempel - ohne - nennenswerte - Kenntnisse.
Frauen gibt man keine Arbeit. sie bezeichnen diese Gesellschaftsform als
H O N K, Humanität of None Kindness. Gesellschaft - ohne Freundlichkeit

The German officials all gone across the board,
up to those, who decide on pensions, and do nothing yourself,
don't want to contribute anything, for all their privileges,
not because they can't, to grant the masses a dignified old age,
but because they don't WANT !

Once i tell you a little story...
Here these are all my interviews that i got...
first of all was the Art Circle from Spain, The3NinesArts, they had taken me
to their inner Circle, as long as it took, and owned my Blog there with my
opinions and paintings,you may see on my website, in english and german !

second time was the fact that i saved a man's life, from his drug and alcohol
addiction caused by a single childhood trauma, today he is in peace, and
works with elderly, and quit with all this, found out that i saved him from
that suicidal way of life, he officially thanked me and apologized for his
Neandertal way to treat all women in all his life before, because his
precortex has missed his encym for empathic reaction on the people. That
punk with his missing empathy was causing some medical advice that i
found out myself, and a seemingly doctor from far, who interviewed me
almost a year, as long as it took to stand by my punker friend and not let him
fall, so that was a successful but hard working issue. The doctor said
spontaneously that i am pretty much a mental and psychic healthy person to
say that i too have an immense power for healing others.

I had my pretty problems with someone who definitely interviewed me the
third time being interviewed. He was an old guy with health and alcohol
problems retired in his wooden house, reading books all the time, with an
old hate on his parents, father slapt and mother ignored him young, he was
from the GDR, so had a definite german hate on all the West, specially their
women. He gave me a huge interview about my thought, and quick these
were two books written. When he had recieved my personal help about his
health and came back from hospital, he changed to a monstrous guy with the
try make me a Christian believer, and told he did that way to all others, that i

65

am no one special. He started to become louder and more aggressive, that i stood and was held by my own protection to still say "No" and saw him in my dream as liar, i am pretty aware of my real fellows who love me in real life. When he decided to explode in front of me, i did a genious trick, don't know how that functioned, but as well as I almost tried to give him a resent answer about his ashole my computer broke down and rested black for three days, then all was good again. So my own PC gave me a protection, not to spend on those people's low level never, to become aggressive ! hihihi - It was real fun. Ah back to that old aggressive Christian his interviews shown in two books. I had heard him explode from far soo alone.

But all those interviews don't make me so happy anymore. It is all too much work. Maybe i am never able to make the other part happy enough to stay friends. I am not the luckiest to keep these contacts alive. Well, as nice people as they say, I can't do more than see myself as energetic, creative and productive. You see, some are good enough to work as doctors a life long and insist without have a private life or family. You see, others are good enough to have chosen the Art of wording to use and help out poorer people as social feeling lawyers that they might come to the rights like the rich, too. You see, there is one like me with a huge experience through life, professionally, artistic have survived so many times, that i had to do art and write not to explode in mind, this life long energy felt had to be canalized and brought out, or i would have to jump the abyss. That was the holy sun that filled me with the energy since i am young, imagine a child stick his little finger in an plug and then feel that unstilled energy from inside to the outside. When that child afterwards comes back onto his feet, the power grows. Sun is everywhere !

Yes, what an ass the father was ! Life is a thing made up of several people.
Dating my mother's partner. Compare other people with it.
These unfortunate creatures. Who can't think of anything else.
Couple love is the weakest love of the universe,
of madness double stupidity for two, divided, love divided, divided into two, happiness only half of everything !

Make peace ! No war !
Guys love go barefeeted.
Guys raise kids alone.
Guys walks all dogs.
Guys call woman and man welcome. amused about those kids,
today run around with the beer, like a baby on mom's breast,
not wanting to make babies, but are sameway ignored, asit in the bushes,
smoke a pipe, waiting for the tic.
I came from the woods, where i found a piece of rubbish,
and took it with outside of it. No power no War is the device !

It was not me who took all the neighborhood dogs out all the time, no it was
the dogs with hunger for freedom likewise who took me out to escape !
No this is not that "Hello, my friend !" nowadays it is not that
"Welcome, i am landing in your arms !" never to try to climb someone's
heart, nor to enter a tall person by "Hello" with smile,
did you know each other, well, if not this is our NORTHERN GERMANY,
and WE ALL DO WHAT WE WANT.

I've always thought that people and voyeurs weigh things up like that and
like to puzzle over the fates of strangers and make judgments like that -
What is more serious about child abuse?

The act of the father sleeping with the woman's daughter, impregnates her,
then kills her mother in front of her, and raises their child as a small family,
although I assume that at some point the impregnated child would no longer
make a sound under his thumb, …

or the father's act, which stimulates the sadistic, violent urges,
on his daughter, with everyone around him witnessing even the mother spies
on her daughter to remove her umbilical cord, the sisters and family
remnants are recruited, to drive away the daughter, to discriminate against
her if she returns, devalue, intimidate, taboo, chase people out the door, try
to listen out, follow into your own life, and their son try to buy things off

with gifts, and to convince of the mother's alleged disorder, with constant control over life, to lure with payment. It is therefore clear that violent abuse in any form is abuse and has consequences, and one assumes that this daughter would not be able to breathe for most of her life, perhaps the spatial separation would enable her to do this from the age of 55 !

Does it need to be mentioned, which type of child abuse would be worse here, or aren't both criminal? According to my theory, all acts of violence committed by fathers against a child are such destructive forces that all others around these culprits also become accomplices and change their character to his bad level, where such a man lies down, as grass no longer grows either.

Every encounter with me as a child,
with a parrot,
with a hard-boiled vinegar egg,
with a tapeworm too,
with one that comes from no matter where
Encounter that wasn't family,
I lived in it,
I only knew one thing,
look into the horse's eyes,
eat his dirt,
rather fall into his dirt,
stink like a goat
and most importantly, BE AWAY!
RUN - RUN – RUN!

Here is a neighbor who choses to just walk barefeeted, he is always soo damn interested in storys about the animal in the neighborhood, now i know why hahahah He is my WALKING INDIAN !
but that man told me in the beginning, to take care, not to just walk like that, because after short a while those feet change, and if you then walk again usually in shoes, you might have a big problem with it.

I rembember when chased off from family, that my winter was so cold had no shoes in winter snow, went inside of an empty cold house, where was a cold stove, and one single cat like me, we laid down and she held me warm, i made a kinda meditation to feel save and warm, and on top of that stove stood a pair of small moccasins, in my size, then i had shoes for the snow outside. No wonder, that i never thought about eating, because this illusion was stuck in that thought of a kinda tuna tin, and the knowledge, if i even stole it, then had no way to open that fucked damn thing, so still no eating, and as well as eating was such a damn difficult thing, my pride grew to never eat anything from anyone as well as he or she would not offer this as friendly gesture ! That is the single reason why wanderers leave the places, because a situation without food, meant to go on, and try at another place far away again anew, then you had many places where you might have felt homy, but so many places in heart like one place, and you feel homy in the huge planet all over the place. You need no vacancy no travel afterwards, because all adventures spin in your rememberings.

So Vacancy in Fantasy,
So free space in the imagination. Find a gap there so that instead of dreaming of full plates of food later, you can enjoy the pleasure of vacation, the memories of which only remain attached to your own dirt, that is why i hide from tourism places so much ! They are spilling their rubbish, shitting aside ways, hanging fat and fed in the sunny chairs, and ask everybody for a gift for the tourist, wanting to enter your home, take all they can as trophy and drive home, then really ask the next year, if they might come back again, free Logie ?

To all tourists! Everyone go to...
SALZGITTER, REMSCHEID or to SAUERLAND!
Everyone always goes there into those financed by the state
KUR - GUESTS there, and the are known for their oblivion,
that's why there are slaughter festivals
always for the greatest satisfaction for a feel-good massage,
PRIVILEGE, released as cured, plus the SOUL WASTE BIN
provided by the masseur, at state expense, mind you !

Today they are eating they complain, they say,
because everyone can say anything,
Politics of tomorrow should be back according to plan
smell like mothballs, the statesman resembles a fish stick,
old men turn to rot, Modernization is rigorously abolished,
Minorities are banned. Women are banned from the language again,
the leadership in office is desecrated,
and taught the brothel some decency again,
reverse turn imitated, Nuclear power accepted again,
Everyone used to love driving cars so much
Working makes everyone "free" again
old racists were still allowed to do everything
limited perception made everyone happy,
when things get better for the old gray men,
even the stupidest will recognize
that the climate works with them,
because if you stand the wrong way,
you can also move forward in reverse gear,
the woman of the south doesn't have to cook,
there's enough sausage stuck to it,
Dad wears the "open fly" again
harass the wife, rarely only sober,
that they don't have time to gender.

Dreams have no morality !
Dreams are a business,
they serve as a value for every fraud,
they pretend to be their fatherly friend,
and just want to be flattered,
even if the liar is an old, unpopular fellow,
at the other end, no Don Quixote at all.
Dreams fail to achieve their goals because
where it was about the light at the end of the tunnel,
and no one had ever dared to go there on foot,
in order to therefore ask others for money,
to reach the goal and end up in bad shoes.
Dreams are not a more beautiful word,
around everyone who wanders along completely outside of morality,
to trigger the shock of the Alps,
and then one-up the monster of fear,
to end the war by paying a sum.
Imagine this business with other people's dreams,
intervenes in a certain sense in everyone's everyday life,
and yet everyone falls for it !

If according to official German people don't know yet
who you are dealing with here since it is easy for him to confirm,
in a society that is structured like this suppress the women, keep them out,
stigmatizing poor people and single parents
to beat the shit out of your own daughters,
or, if necessary, to deprive them of their child, using enormous force,
BECAUSE YOU CAN - if you don't know here yet,
what clan of old men, old men, on their sinking ship,
remember what's left here LAST STATEMENT
of a power that has remained thin, and whose desires cling to indulging,
who knows how to choose in any case.
TIP – THEY FUCK ON CARRION !
I CAN GIVE HIM MY TOILET PAPER sufficient !

Equality for women
freedom of speech
regulated in the statute book
is not sausage based
the woman is not a minority in this country
not to convert the people in the country
the allergy to missionary position is immense
the young people experience skin allergy to it
a first lady doesn't let herself be a henpecked man
make the breakfast rolls in the morning,
The city dwellers themselves are not considered a minority !

The man wants to hunt, that I don't laugh !
Can't see the forest for the trees.
The woman cannot escape his eyes.
Sees one lying behind every bush. It hardly gives him any rest.
Giving in to the desire to shoot, faithful to the senses yet indiscriminate,
surrender to his power, stalked, don't take away the peace of the forest,
stares at the woman, in the image of his mother bitch,
as if he could commit it in the middle of the street,
giving her the coup de grace. His weapons speak for themselves.
In every type of hunt, it's important to find it.
Who opens the mouth to educate the youth, actually doesn't do anything else
sending inexperienced people alone into the forest at night,
who should finally discover nature for themselves,
instead of just hiding under the down.

The marten does not roam far from the nest.
His motive lay where the perpetrator lived.
The rabbit lives in the fox's den. The hen also broods a foreign egg,
A false bird put this into her. The hunter was once the huntress himself.
He grabbed a cart, transported two cans of beer inside,
and posed in the daily routine, grabbed his daily ready meal,
the direction of the questions doesn't matter to him.
That's hunter language. You shouldn't understand that.

Just had a hilarious conversation.
The nice Mani from Emden introduced himself to me in the countryside.
A great guy, we talked about "working life"! I said I was qualified in all
things medical, in my opinion, to work with old people, in spa clinics as a
masseur and lifeguard, and to work educationally with disabled people,
regardless of their disability and age. Except that in addition to all the
courses and training I learned, I only worked as a voluntary employee
throughout my life, being sent away every now and then without a contract,
but working for years without pay, until the end when I tried to go to the
employment office for help to look for work. I was just in an applicant
course when I introduced myself to everyone in such a way that it all
seemed too stupid to me and that's why I was going to work on a publication
of my experiences from now on, but they cheekily blackmailed me out of
my place from now on working as forced laborers with disabled people, also
without pay, or being a single parent on the street. I did this again as a
volunteer for years, and then at the age of 50 I was sent home from the
church with basically no employment contract, because thanks to my
qualifications I knew how to deal with disabled people perfectly from a
technical point of view, and I was told that I was "overqualified" for them
too Church and instead of a job as too expensive, sent home with a disability
pension, and bye. Hahahaha and what did the mani tell me??? He was
employed in Emden as a public employee in the social center and job center
until he actually expressed an effort to job seekers to get them real
employment. He was then forbidden to do that, he said that because it wasn't
his job in the job center to get people into work.

They should only be put off for the statistics with the help of the applicant courses and turned into long-term unemployed, the placement in work takes a long time no longer their program and intention. Because of this, Mani was not made a civil servant, but he was asked to retire at the age of 50, as I was back then, so only for him was a disability pension and bye-bye, and he was described as "too expensive" for the system. I also personally knew a politician from the Kiel state parliament with a congenital hearing problem who, like me, wanted to fulfill his dream of working with disabled people. He completed the long path to becoming a special needs teacher and asked for work at the local school for children with disabilities. He was rejected because his hearing impairment made him unsuitable for dealing with disabled children. Only then did he complete his studies in politics and law, and went into politics to first draw attention to the fact that disabled people are often not supposed to be helped by competent people, simply because the church considers qualified people to be too expensive, and so on Experienced career changers like me, who know straight away what's going on and say it out loud, are simply undesirable, and only house mothers or ex-soldiers who look after the disabled pro forma, along the edge of everything in washing, feeding and workshops, there's nothing going on but these people to manage as if they no longer had needs.

THAT PROVES people in germany are running like a hare for work, and never succeed,no matter how qualified they are,ZICK ZACK and OUT! Sothat the WILLING of our german country never IS or WAS, a realistic social system, and even our CHILDREN never were welcome at all !

A good guy, who only works for free, and only does good, is no longer like one watery cucumber, from the others pinned in a pickle jar. Their fuss about..."Altruism" "Self-sacrifice" and "buoyancy"as ridiculous as one Horde of people locked starve humanly in it, and take their own lives, and never was my destiny !

I just say to everyone...which involve discrimination
try to participate is like bad sex, accept, "Oh, that wasn't a career move!"
or "Eh, like ejaculate on the jacket!" and "have fun with it !"

More rudeness than expected ! Gynecological
Denunciation is not a concept, that has proven itself...
the question, how do you undress? The tension dramatic effect,
you do not give birth knowingly to give them the joy
while you put in your effort, your soon-to-be-born dream child,
including authorization withdrawal, to steal just as undignified,
mistreat, abuse, torture for the fun of a company, deeper than you think...
whether you have children in this country is really that pleasant?
I definitely have didn't make the decision difficult
not to give birth to any more children in this federal state,
or would that have deserved PRAISE in comparison?

I have sometime gave up the horse owner,
already had as a young woman
eaten enough dirt, like that by default!
I have sometime let the piano play be,
because hands you hit they soon fail at playing.
I have sometime the art of healing hung on the nail,
because there is such a thing in this country no registered profession per se,
is no real study per se.
I have sometime the stupid princes nailed to the wall
and left hanging, why leave a comment?
I have sometime let the old die alone, after I looked with what laughter
my grandma died sarcastically and openly, because she knew my life.
I have sometime just let sleep be, because my child went out as an upright
person, avoiding the city where he grew up,
because the anti-social people never go out !
I have sometime the low level of Christians rejected,
that I'm not ready to accept, because I love myself way too much !

The idiot of the year...
should indeed be removed from the chamber,
the dark dungeon, the smell of the pig,
the closet of dark desires, brassiere discarded in the wardrobe,
the parental desert climate, the prickly great aunt hedge,
the naked chicken on a white plate,
tcha, the same idiot should...let everyone fall for everyone's pleasure,
the covers in due course, in the heat flash of the lightning,
with one in the crown, so to speak...
Be part of it for ONE DAY and do the talking,
to influence the lower level, to confirm the group in knowing,
that also a few cans of stale beer, her goal is to make friends will go wrong !

For example, I know when I am mindful, relaxed and sleeping in peace, that my dreams are soft and black and white. Only when I'm looking for inner peace and miss looking at happy faces do I dream in color to find their faces as best I can.

It is a bit strange. If those who commit an offense against the child so that everyone in the family knows about it and deny it, continue the taboo war of annihilation against the child throughout their life, instead of once declaring the horror null and void, and coming out guilty if they do it after 60 years still publicly declare that this is a war of annihilation against her family, that she has to admit her guilt ! HAHAHAHAHAHA, they would still baptize themselves as Jews and feel that they were being treated unfairly, or would declare themselves victimized as Nazis. I always tell my newest autistic friend, "Be brave, my boy! You only speak when you want, you don't justify yourself, you have the time you need, you have the protection of your parents! And know the place of family Not having to leave is always a haven of peace for you. Know that I myself have never entertained the thought of being at a man's side, not wanted, not sought, not experienced, not started, never, and if If I now, at the age of 60, claim to have survived all this alone, then you can definitely do it!"

When you say, A beautiful woman makes the man to the good lover,
then says, a smart woman makes the man to the good critic,
but then one beautiful and smart woman makes every man UNSAFE !

IMMORTAL
an Insta doll...
is active"
always "positive"
drives men crazy with charms
plays the "beautiful" and "smart" woman
who believes at seventeen
that the world is at your feet
without family support
misses looking at happy faces
dreams in color
to make it easier to find friends outside
improved her appearance
makes her a princess
because grandpa told her that
her goal is to create "friends".
that bring in money
Her appearance So the "JACKPOTT" of her life!

S - See your goal
U - Understand the obstacles
C - Create a positive mental pic
C - Clear your mind of self-doubt
E - Embrace all challenges
S - Sacrifice free time
S - Show you can do it
F - Feed your focus
U - Utilize all opportunities
L - Learn from all failures.

BACKFISH nonsense!
They want to be loved. Admire the warrior.
They judge him harshly, who doesn't give them love.
They become cruel because of this,
because they have a different perception.
They do not feel their iniquity, since they can't,
has nothing to do with the will to do so.
They are only trapped in the ego for so long,
that only revolves around her,
As long as they are called narcissists.
Until they commit a sword deed, then they killed first,
and are given the middle name psychopath.

Where such a one lies down,
Grass no longer grows !

Men are good at something...
always what they imagine
but in reality only bungling can do it,
like raising your own four walls,
The top model should then grow up in it,
who you tear the laundry off,
the elevation for the house in question,
said another, who was later said to have
that he sexually ambushes young people in the family.
This is how they value being a father,
they could do that incredibly well,
look down on themselves and praise the good piece.
That's why the daughter found "walls"
and to leave them in dangerous situations,
and to escape through the window if necessary.

Life has no guarantees.
Everyone knows that.
But what can be said
that some people see things
which are not like that at all.
And also that there are things in Germany...
for example a Nazi problem, that they don't even see !

Is it an elite partner? let's be honest, in point Old white men,
looking for a mature age... Landed a tad too far to the right?

Then.... now we will contribute something to enlightenment...!
This little corner finally grows, the soft pussy knows what it is,
the pussy secretion flows, it goes in and out again,
and according to the description... We will always do this in the future
a positive experience out of it, as often as possible, and with whom,
but there is no guarantee, some people do better comfortable in life alone.

Men are no longer in great demand as they get older, which makes them
ambivalent, grumpy and more incapable of criticism than they would like.
That's why these clients use the networks to take revenge on women. To use
the untraceability and anonymity of the Internet to play on their whims, to
harm people, and to shake people's ideas of the good in people, to force
them to question and doubt their own lives. They always invent the same
false resumes and fake characters that contradict the truth. So they are not
good in bed, they appear as the Spanish Quixote. If they are reluctant to go
into depth when it comes to women, they describe themselves as having
always been scientifically interested in the natural beliefs of the Indians, and
in reality they are in shabby shoes and would not want to hike a meter far
with a woman they are friends with I would have liked to have taken her as
my wife 30 years earlier for a wonderful time.
Where the origin they chose is not described in detail because they have no
idea about the mentioned country they associate themselves with since they
cannot even admit to understanding the native language of the country.

Although these old gentlemen, that's what I'll call them, in reality none of them are the doctors they think they are, they mostly use the Texas origins, are about 55 years old, are extremely professionally committed to saving people, and use the same dubious ones Online bank accounts to which they demand large donations, they are actually all orphans who were adopted by a Catholic family, either their wife or both parents have already died, and they always mentioned their only daughter was just ten and would be in Hawaii or a Catholic boarding school, and she has a heart defect, poor thing, which makes it impossible to come for a visit; it is not possible for her daughter to travel due to her health. Where these guys suspect that we already know about this orphan scam and the attempt to steal all of their savings from people who have been through hardship themselves and are considered disadvantaged and who shouldn't be tried in the name of charity. As soon as they read this in their supposed native language understanding, they immediately tuck in their tails or are so bold as to claim that the "trouble" of entertaining has been going on for so long and there has been no reward for them. Or they had the trick of exploring people's triggers in the service of self-enrichment in order to woo them in the wrong image and to offend them, almost to stalk them, to awaken hope again until the first nightmares awaken and the people It is easier to come under pressure in a short process in order to steal their money, i.e. to "crack" them psychologically for money, as they say. It deals with all the consequences for people in a limitless and unscrupulous manner, with the intention of acting to their greatest possible harm, of daring to continue the same thing in every conceivable way via email years later. All you need to do is go to the police and file a report, that will shut things down and stop accessibility. Every woman who speaks openly about such cases of fraud realizes that she has given away money and in return only received the memory of a zero eight fifteen cheapest proposal, not even from Texas, and in all likelihood from fraudsters from the Holland neighborhood , perhaps also Belgium, by people who are not the least bit linguistically competent but can brazenly lie. Anyone can lie, Hans and Franz and Hinz and Kunz, it's the business world of psychopaths.

I am back to where it all began, meditation, breathing, sage smoking, lavender perfum, visualizing, inner issues, transformation, wisdom, empathy, protection, my inner ancestors, those who were warriors, grounding, bonding, love, ... that's all.

Do you want me to tell you how they describe aging women like that, with all the hatred they have on their bodies? The word designation also comes from sign, or marked, for example, when a person who is intolerable in the immediate vicinity, suffers from whatever mental illness, that considered intolerable! As a child, I knew the term for such conspicuous things: "she has the smallpox!" as if I can see it in her face today, that when she is forced to look people in the eyes, red swams of blood appear on her face. Buddhists would describe these as people who had a certain liver disease that destroyed their liver, as if such an uncomfortable woman would always have to walk hunched over, carrying a small trolley in her hand with the constant daily ration of cheap canned beer in it, because these people are so much hate that it is already destroying their liver. The doctors actually prescribe such women blood thinners so that people can tell that if she actually looks you in the eyes at that moment, her anger shoots out of her face like blood shooting out of the nose, and that's exactly what happens.

Your mind is a powerful thing.
The Four Noble Truths
Stay away from the fools !

Your joy at the happiness of others,
is perhaps the most beautiful thing today, what was left to us
and fleeting as the tidal winds, and yet to discover again every day,
and to awaken the other again,
because happiness and magic are in everyone !

My breakfast is not sausage in the morning, but an apple is good for health. I've been reducing meat consumption for a long time. I usually replace sugar with substitutes, Since I know that sugar is not a natural food, and threatening, it not only forms diabetes one day, but accumulates a fatty structure that triggers a constant hunger effect in the brain, and obesity causes you to "starve". I always eat whole grain bread, or cereal muesli with freshly crushed grain, which is actually just filling, even since I know that people's intestinal collapse comes from wheat flour. The same is true for the ingredients of all ready-made meals and all the sauces you buy are very stressful for the liver. Advertised oils with saturated fatty acids are unusable and are also present in ice cream. As we know that sugar and fat in a product multiply each other's bad effects, alcohol also causes the so-called fatty liver. Any diet that goes on quickly is not good for the body and doesn't pay off, because what you take from your body quickly, it will soon get back twice as much !

Freshly ground coffee, stored away from light, green tea, daily fruit, even if only 1 apple per day, grains, sufficient seasoning of the food, with Asian spices such as cardamom, coriander, curry, garlic, allspice, chilli, paprika, nutmeg, etc ., nuts and linseeds, whose good fats are necessary for physical development and breakdown, the immune system and the balance in blood sugar and are particularly good for the heart vessels. I have been consuming protein via soy every day for more than 20 years. I can only afford good eggs in exceptional cases, I don't afford such luxuries as healthy, lean meat or expensive salmon. Elegant, valuable oils such as coconut oil, natural olive oil, cold-pressed avocado oil are not for my wallet, but are intended for salads as an exception. I also can't afford valuable fish; most fish these days have too high a concentration of heavy metals and good fish is too expensive.

Alcohol destroys the complexity of the body in many places, liver vessels become fatty, then poisons can no longer be excreted, heart vessels become clogged, digestion loses its ability to absorb valuable nutrients and proteins into the body, so poison accumulates, destroys all body cells and leaves the person almost starve. It opens the door to many other chronic illnesses. The immune defense is ineffective.

Salt must be natural and in moderation, otherwise it causes high blood pressure and heart problems, the small vessels in all organs are vital and dangerous in the event of a heart attack, including the brain or liver, the lymphatic vessels and digestion. If these vessels are destroyed by aggressive salts, everything collapses, even water accumulates in the tissue because the lymphatic system fails, which endangers the circulation due to an imbalance in the water balance. I also don't drink any fruit juices because their good effect in juice concentrate without the pulp is too demanding and when concentrated it seems too sweet, just as vitamin preparations are much more likely to have a toxic effect if overdosed.

Living healthily also means living joy, who knows how long it will last. The mind is a tremendous power. So use it and don't follow the idiots.

I never thought I was crazy, like they told me.
I wasn't told I should be loved, no matter.
I was rather told I am not lovable to them.
I didn't wait for love. I didn't expect love.
I didn't experience love.
But if I had had that chance,
that everyone I liked would have loved me,
then I wouldn't have been crazy,
just because i am not a follower of the fools.

YESS, this is sooo easy ! With those blind spots in Justice !
Have hired the own one lawyer, and WUPPS the injustice solves,
and WUPPS turns out into dust, so EASILY, you understood....
this is the new german way to finding justice nowadays,
it takes years to suffer, and to help you out on your own,
kinda walk on the egde until to be seen, wether you eat the dust, or...
to get through their principles...and WUPPST they are sooo sudden gone,
those PRINCIPLES...and your issue found justifying,
then it becomes public that the TRUTH is being said.

The discussion includes men,
are they more dangerous to women than bears?
Are you not wrong in assuming that
that bears are far more harmless,
instead men look more like giant crocodiles?
Which young person has not already suffered failure?
who no longer wants sex with anyone of her species in the evening?
will go even further, we are North Germans here,
that everyone has learned at some point that men are violent criminals,
they cannot be wiped off the map, have always been before,
that a "greeting" in the north has always been the case just the irony of it!
Every woman's greeting contains it can be scanned,
whatever violence she might encounter.
I know two girls who have their ripcord thanks to me
have pulled, with a very light blow
on the back of her head and a loving push
recognized that they had been the prince's followers.

Do you know how to recognize that someone has no style?
On the hairstyle? No.... he is ignorant and stupid,
all his actions come from to hurt someone else with every act,
especially the old, weak and children,
That means, "He steps down... to show his superiority !"

If someone had a strange dream of me, but as it often is, did not feel strange,
he was ... "in a huge cave with people walking around like ants, without a
sign of a subway car, like i know them from work, but i was there working
on something. But suddenly i was with you in a corridor and you were
pregnant and about to give birth through very calm and without any sign of
pain. I asked if there was anything i could do. You said, no nothing, no
problem. I have done this before you know, and then said, I only was there
to film it."

Funny but truly strange.

I had seen today on the meadow a young happy couple hugging asit closely, that I said "What happiness to be ! There is nothing above !" and asked if they too had babies in between ? Then the lady showed me her pregnant belly so proud and in her friends arms held. We spoke about the wonder of relationship of a Mom and her beautiful daughter, in another way like with her son. I said to her "Don't worry. If there is birth. Hurts sure. But no problem, afterwards she is forgetting all in one second and is really High like on drugs for a whole week !" So this to be pregnant. She was happy about our talk, and she is prepared now not to agree in a so-called cesarean section, because i told her this is a pure business thought of the hospital, and she said, that she will take care ! and as well as you altime dream in being in caves, this is not so bad, i find this is a kinda ancient thing.

You know that two days ago i dreamed of such a cave too, with lots of big big crocodiles, then went to a beach to be alone, and thought that i usually would not hide to swim in every water i see, but by that thought of the big crocodiles i hesitated. This meant a small cut in the belly and just take the baby out by the surgeons. This is the very successful way of hospitals nowadays not to wait longer, that babies arrive their natural ways, they just decide this above the bearing mom, and do it for their own profite, because one natural born baby gives them profit 10.000 € and one cesaresan section give the hospital 30.000 € plus in a much shorter time.

I dreamed of talking to a platttysk old man, him speaking in his dialect, and then dreamed of the secret signs of the cyrillic wordings with the inhold of the medicine thought, and i dreamed of the own seen map of North Germany. With that thought after that night i sat in front of my neurologist for my medicine, he is young studied and russian, and we had a fight about diagnosis, and how to treat people like me, and rapist, and respect, then he wanted me to learn russian, i really tried, but doesn't work. You see that i am arriving here in the north, i feel more and more like a nordic woman. I know my identity to be one of the nordic here. Sothat i would tell each one, even my worst enemy all what i directly had to tell, and nothing but that. Straight true words. Maybe i felt to be taken down into your inner caves too strong or often, that i needed distance, not to be stuck in it. Life is to find out the way in and out of each ones personal caves by him alone.

That is funny ! I really had those days my several feelings to bear one new baby in my belly, like the little daughter in me, carried around. When Dan Magnus Lundgren that swedisch friendly guy spoke to me... When someone had a strange dream about me but, as often happens, didn't feel strange about it, they were... "in a huge cave with people walking around like ants, with no sign of a subway car, like." at work, but I was there working on something and you were pregnant and about to give birth, completely calm and with no signs of pain. I asked if there was anything I could do. Your answer was - No, nothing, no problem. I've done this before, as you know, and then I said - I was just there to film it."

Funny, but really strange. Today I saw a young, happy couple on the meadow, hugging each other so tightly that I said: "What happiness! There's nothing to top it off!" and asked if they'd had babies along the way? Then the lady proudly showed me her pregnant belly while the guy was holding his girlfriend in his arms. We talked about the miracle of the relationship between a mother and her wonderful daughter, in a different way than with her son. I told her, "Don't worry. When birth occurs. So that means not agreeing to a so-called cesarean section, because I told her it was purely a business policy of the hospital and she said she would take care of it! This means a small incision in the abdomen and the surgeons simply removing the baby. This is the very successful method used by hospitals these days to stop waiting for babies to be born naturally. They simply decide about the birthing mother and do this for their own benefit, because a naturally born baby brings them a profit of €10,000 and one through a cesarean section gives the hospital €30,000 more in a much shorter time.
And although sometimes you dream about being in caves, it's not that bad, I think it's a pretty ancient thing. You know that two days ago I also dreamed of such a cave with lots of big crocodiles, then went to a beach to be alone and thought that normally I wouldn't hide swimming in the water, but at this thought of what I saw... I hesitated about the big crocodiles.

I dreamed of being with an old man in Platttysk who spoke in his dialect, and then I dreamed of the secret symbols of the Cyrillic formulations with the corresponding influence of medical thought, and dreamed of my own map from Northern Germany. With this thought I sat in front of my neurologist after that night. He is young, educated and Russian, and we argued about the diagnosis and how to treat people like me badly, but not their rapists, and demanded respect from me, then he wanted me to start learning Russian, but it doesn't work . You see that I arrive here in the north, I feel more and more like a Nordic woman. I know that I am one of the Nordic people here.

So that I would tell everyone, even my worst enemy, everything that I had to say directly and nothing but that. Downright true words. When I see my neurologist friend again, I'll keep a bundle of my innermost thoughts here, translated into his language. But to come back to your cave dream. Maybe I felt like I was being pulled too hard into your inner caverns or often that I needed space to avoid getting stuck in there. Life consists of finding the way into each individual's personal caves alone.

Let me introduce you today "THE WOLVER!"

- pronounced "VULVA" testifies to the innermost of the inner -
contemporary from the view of the husky behind the dike
right up to the Middle Ages, the smooth transition stopped briefly
over the railway line to the field straight over past the father's monument,
into the blue algae lagoon the garden fence of the schoolyard into the field
the leaf lettuce is numerically large, across the valley into the wild garlic
knee-deep in the swamp of those left behind
rugged rock on the edge of the wood on the highest tree on the mountain
the ten ducks behind after the dwarf, no lush meadow further into the valley
around the female figures at the castle hiked to the kingfisher and....
whoever knows the name of him, he should have a crumb in his coffee
in the morning after the tour have received !

Practical long-term statistics ! Praktische Statistik auf Langzeit !
It is not uncommon for diverse women to become viewed as a side entrant.
So the church not only accommodates women,
employed across the board as a socially committed example.
If the country goes further, those to whom they do not give green card work,
who therefore still hire themselves out
for nothing and without remuneration,
as those who do not preserve the gear,
comparatively like that, with contracts,
which they can collectively bully out for it!
It is even said that the mills grind slowly,
me from trained profession to profession,
temporarily allowing people to work for free,
that it shows the number of professional internships,
that I don't belong to the working class at all,
knowing that the army of the unemployed is like that
don't even have the means to complain about it.
There are mushrooms big and small, say the disabled,
I was the lucky guy to be your client,
the management of the workshops
had been missing you for a long time,
also because there are still social people like me,
who do work for the sake of it,
and not the colleagues bullying for the salary,
who seem overqualified to you !
I'm just wondering why all this?
As is well known, it is not new that in the social sector
far more employees are required,
but they are not paid and forced out of work,
So the focus is on caring for people,
the therapeutic approach for the disabled
not possible due to a lack of staff, which is unfortunate.

A country like Germany,
that is so anti-social with job seekers,
qualified, committed, adaptable, life-experienced,
citizens of the country, exploiting her and kicking her ass
rushed through offices and defamed,
she still tries to proselytize, so to speak, whatever that means.
This country should still be amazed
that an army of slaves for life NOT READY FOR THIS
for organ donations themselves to have to serve voluntarily,
what a FARCE else the CREAM on the COFFEE WOULD BE !

Isn't it the German philistine?
Afraid it could happen to him on the operating table
something to be taken, even though they aren't dying?
Imagine if a German would in case of death,...
took the ORGAN cell phone?
This shows immense fear of loss.
Of course.

Who to expect? Not any you would want. They act and be.
and have names, and titles, and shit in their pants
and you might know them for long.
I ask myself, "Who would come running the first person I told
You can transplant my eggs, let's see what's for you this year still comes out
I can see his face really vividly imagine,
like him on all fours for it came crawling to me ! och, as well as their
missing reputation forces them to come crawling, and begging and bow in
front of you.... this takes about three and half years.
Where are the principles?
Overfishing in Europe large commercial catch
quintupled and illegal ones at Fish stocks declined in 50 years 70%
- we will see,
where their shark fish soup leads !

My name is HAI-KE or HEI-KE,
I was never respected as a woman,
than this, which I am, about my desire to have children
I just said it is prevented in this country
that children are only born, because birth is equated with
Shark alarm, and overfishing,
That's why our wishes for children are ignored.
But who asked me about it,
just the last 27 years? - no one there !

will soon be valid in Germany for all women,
only commercial childbearing, Ritsch Ratsch,
artificially inseminated, Caesarean section, cropped short, hung on the drip,
shown to the woman get your tits out, EI-Der-Daus,
where is the hammer hanging?

Will a woman learn to defend herself by inviting friends who confirm that
her neighborhood and home peace are being disturbed? Anyone who is
supposed to help her must refrain from the partnership, put his own interests
aside, and make his contribution without taking into account the initiation of
a relationship. I'll try it. It would simply take a witness statement, I
appreciate the certain times when the neighbor is guaranteed to cause
trouble. That's early in the morning, right in the quiet midday hour and
exactly at night when it's time to go to bed. I know someone I like, I'll visit
him tomorrow morning and explain this to him. He's already said that it's
good for me to defend myself. It's good to stick with people who are adults
when there are such everyday disturbances and disturbances to the peace in
the house in order to get rid of any inconveniences. The lawyer also advised
me that it would make this matter easier and she said we would know how
to deal with it better when she came back from vacation.

Suicide is not a solution to anything. Think positive, ahhh yes for sure, the trees around would shout on me, the friend i meet in the woods would also, my dog would not be amused, so not my son, who stands alone then, my intellect thrown to dirt would not be amused, my intellect still wants wonders and happiness, i see every abyss i stood before, and my strong believe, that suicide is just a quick illusion to fail in life, i am aware. Very well, good reasons to obtain happiness, and live life as it should be lived. Ohh yess, i just think about that lady lawyer, when she made me strong believe again in sunshine of the better side of life, then her special low price she made for me, and she already joins now in a wonderful holiday, and soon wants to see me back, with her advices, she made. Then we continue.

First person i met to ask, and tried to explain me, he said, that he is a burned child, and we did not know us for a couple of years before, he did nothing for a stranger, that he cannot trust to pay me with his solidarity. But the second person i visited then after him, we do know us since more than twenty years as sympathic people, and he is definitely giving me his guarantee, that from now on there is hope at the other end of the way to see, and he feels that solidarity, ufff we ARE FRIENDS:
YES DEAR, now the summer may come ! A witness is found !

Reference:
To my statement, I would also like to attach the testimony of a friend.

We have known each other for more than twenty years.
I can definitely trust his statement. He was willing to be present in my apartment several times to get an idea of what Mrs. S. arranged over me, to get on the last nerve of me and the old dog at my side, i.e. to disturb the peace and quiet at home. R.M. was present and it was clear to both of us that that Ms.S. for example during the midday rest period
between 12:00 noon to around 1:00 p.m
disturbing the peace by moving furniture around,
always moving or dropping objects while restless, shutters open and close
often use the toilet flush, dishes rattle,sometimes causes things to fall loudly

So my old dog in particular, who needs peace and quiet in the middle of the day in the heat of the day and is looking for sleep, leaves the rooms completely anxious and panicked. Where Ms.S. is just going on, the dog is filled with fear and clings to me, looking at the ceiling, then it takes a long time for the dog to calm down.

Then Ms.S runs. suddenly out of the house,
finally runs back upstairs to her apartment 5 minutes later,
three times in a row, locking her apartment with multiple locks.
Lately I've noticed that I'm woken up early in the morning by their loud bangs. I feel a tornado of noises at intervals and for hours at night,
right after I lock the door and want to go to rest. She gets into it as soon as I don't defend myself, that is, if I don't call the police to knock on her door.

Ms.S. is perhaps subconsciously aware that her behavior has been known for a long time, documented and corresponds to facts, that I am now seeking help and that she was warned by me. Nevertheless, it can be observed that her clinical picture drives her into the arms of religiously dubious people. Such a person waited in front of my front door early in the morning and threw a threatening Bible verse at me without identifying himself. Since such influence is not good for the psyche of an unstable woman like Ms.S. is, and probably only increases her paranoidity, is obvious. According to the testimony of my acquaintance R.M. it can be observed that Ms.S. is in an increasing state that is dangerous to others - and perhaps also to itself.

Kind regards, Schleswig, May 17, 2024, Heike Thieme

You see, to be in touch with the people even with some only twenty five years long on the road every days, makes you sure one single day, that you would need them, that is the reason why i said that so often to people, not to live isolated. Nothing comes from Nothing. I have found a friend. There is hope for the end of that way. He will witness this. And my lawyer will be happy after holiday. Thankxxxx for holding on to me !

EASY TO SEE ON ANY REGIONAL MAP!
Whose father pays well for school,
Donations, home care, Club contributions, children's language courses,
Old people's association funds, death insurance,
Hercules monument preservation, animal protection association,
school club, civil service music school, Dog sports club German Shepherds,
Shooting range, Bavarian culture festival, Hunter's Latin and shooting club,
Tennis leisure, the confirmation group, and the local round club, ...
yes, he might have a chance the following statement,
which is to be made publicly, ...

"We prefer to keep our children well lubricated, healthy and stupid, and
keep it that way. Because voting is only fair for those over 18,
because it cannot be supported, let the stupid people vote!"

People marry rich for money. Not a word in the world language, however,
starts with a T - and ends with a T!
So if the world language is not agrees with every other language,
a woman wanted to claim her little child from someone else's cuckoo,
laying in his bed would be a smart move? But society wants it,
that women can calculate like that, throw themselves into business,
as if it had to be compensated with footwork,
that this petty guilt of sex work, claims itself as a tolerated loan,
that she never truly studies, had tried hard and worked.
If these Neanderthal girls though swing the club for the rest of your life,
How do you look at the village you live in? I would say, the people there
wouldn't even get to know them, or never knew any of them in pretty paint,
seen, viewed as the center, or ever received a positive sign from them.
Isn't that the main reason for me never to get involved in a partnership?
We live in a very unhealthy world, we have to live so we don't get infected.
Good day, yes, but that lets me think more complex about how to trust into
each other, when people try to engage in partnership, and have such evil
thought how to cheat their partners or destroy, that meant not to get infected
by inhumanity.

How can friends and men seem to be loyal if people watch them treat their partners really unfair ?

This is altime my part to wait and when time has come even after 20 years, to bring that issue on the plate and let them finally know, so slow and soft, but direct and true. A person with any handicap or one with any life chosen, and owning nothing but the knife in their pockets, won't let me know, that unfairness would be legal to me. And you said it, to once accept bad characteristic behaviour and ignore the victim, and let it like that and ignore, gives the bad seeds in ones own heart, with no good consequences to live in a lie. THE REAL SICKNESS IN LIFE ARE LIES.

If a woman decides for her heart, to save my life,
by killing a person, and always regretted it,
but cleared the way for me, to leave her there,
where evil has been done to people,
then their actions have meaning devoted to me,
to whom this is attributed, to burn on his fur,
who planned an existence for me,
that I should have ended up like that woman.

If it was the last of me, to help an innocent person
and I've learned to live with it, then that's okay,
then that's what I do !

A truly evil man once said in the sight of the daughter,
who never liked him, didn't need, didn't appreciate
didn't pay attention, didn't honor
when father didn't want to
only when she was unclothed
lay threshed in front of him,
"WHAT A WASTE!"

LOVE IS NOT THE MEANING OF ALTRUISM.

Everyone wants to be loved. Not one of them understands, first in order to become a loved one you yourself have to understand how to love. The search for Great Love is as futile as not embodying love itself. Which people always want to belong to someone or something, they are also used and treated like underage children, they swear that they are heart and heart, and a heart makes both into a whole, but who but them wants to know that? People paint people's pictures. It is usually your oil portrait of individual figures in a life situation, but always one model alone. This makes it clear that everyone wants to be seen, appear present, step off the wall and be admired. Only if you go to a museum to take part in oil portraits and nudes and drawings in life, there would be no closeness.

How many people expose themselves in pole dancing? How many people make their money in the porn business? They may live financially independently, but in an isolated world in which they only pretend to be close, caring, longing, and sexual fulfillment. There are no feelings of love there on either side. If women in their emerging age are irritated that love offers no guarantee in the market of feelings,

then LOVE IS NOT THE MEANING OF ALTRUISM.

As much as they long for it one last time in their old age, their old injuries make them thin-skinned. It's good to determine at an early stage what real skills you're aiming for, to assess the person you're dealing with, to scan them yourself first. Before the other person does the same to you and you fall for them. If the crisis from one's youth would open up as a trap in one's approaching age, seeing the same chaotic conditions experienced arise, then the emotions surprise you very much, the surprise of your own tears, anger and extreme laughter becomes a test of finally learning to get yourself under control, or of being torn from your calm by a series of nightmares with a traumatic origin. You can never know when such a reappraisal of previous crises in life will arise, but then attention is required, and caution, and mindfulness in dealing with your own life in order not to slip on this emotional wave. You usually fall for yourself and deceive yourself and the world into thinking that someone else is to blame for your own fate!

In life there is not always a mother's hand there to protect you and bring you back to the haven of peace. This is what adulthood entails. And everyone has to be on their guard when it comes to love!

It's better not to play masochism.
Not everyone has the courage to do that.
It's not always the case that someone wants to stalk.
Not the other one who is prepared for "help".
There are no roots strong to build the bridge.
Not the horsepower to have met someone like that.
The greatest healing power rarely lies in love.
No success without a medical background.
It is absolutely impossible to make an angel out of others.
With your sacrifice, the friendship will not continue.
but that's where everything will end,
where masochism ends in despair,
where no one will take you out then,
where the healer meets his own death!

Yesterday a youngster ran past us the entire Berliner Straße
up and down again I was already in bed, the boy sang in Ukrainian
his song of praise to love
his love song to peace
his fight song against Russia
his ode to summer
his passionate delight
at all like we ALL be alive
and to be able to live in freedom !

PRINCIPLES; which disappear over the course of YEARS or MONTHS !
I don't have the ambition either to help those who falling short in love,
mentally injured people without good examples,
exemplary limited stuck people,
party lions without any significant knowledge,
problematic, erotically out of line,
begging for wellness, asking for Aunt Emma's cake,
then Uncle George's cigar smoking, the ashtrays to saute,
not even suitable for a German woman,
which statically stands in the app for Looser, still confuse the harbor tour
with an Ikea scented candle in purple or turquoise,
So the Ikea inspired ones of a lifelong marriage.

WHERE ARE THE PRINCIPLES ??? THE PRINCIPLES ARE GONE !!
All is not yet lost. The principle of forbearance remains.
German foresight is the idea of survival !

It was the strawberry's fault
that his girlfriend gave birth to a child,
In Las Vegas the trick prevails,
most people haven't seen him
there are pensioners sitting in a circle at the table,
waste their time and donate money,
today we just call the strawberry bunny,
when the child was unseen bigger,
could do it magic and with one
sign a light with a lighter,
Clearly the lighter was stolen from him!
We emphasize from this,
what blooms for children growing up in poverty,
they either play with wood, stone and paper
build their world on their own computers,
or steal their own toys !

Some people are considered laughingstocks.
Only that they have every cell phone,
get every PC cracked, in 5 minutes, are always on drugs
but never have anything to eat at home.
Just because they need people around them,
and because being alone is difficult for psychos,
they do every dirty job, for fries with chicken, and kebab and a beer.

I have just made a walk around through 46 different human characters
again, who stumble through the world, this ain't just fun to most people, for
sure they kill and abuse, and follow the fools.

Isn't it already too late, just before the collapse to think about health?
When the doctor says, "less salt, meat, tobacco,
less stress, no alcohol !" then it is announced
that the body has suffered multiple damages,
and the risk of a heart attack has increased,
the chance of survival has irreparably reached the lowest level !
The idea of survival in general is important right now.

When the party is loud. Then the friend ran over.
Even if she called out too. Nobody gave her an answer.
If he himself killed her husband ?
Then the cousin himself sank to his knees.
When mom knows life. She didn't know the perpetrators themselves.
If the helper, if the seeker, if the maternal instinct
but she is not a know-it-all.

Queen, she's locked up like my mother in a world full of lies.

Intelligent girls don't come to paradies, they come everywhere,
without being caught in family happiness for eternity, hi, hii !
No negativity could hold you down, if you didn't allow it to get inside you.

All the way back to eternal love for ever. I said that just once, before I searched the next way under a different sky into next big city. Like this woman I once found, I had the same start in literature, when I searched stories in the garbage, I found some, who got lost some times like my baby.

Somewhere out there, a tree tireless producing oxygen,
so you can breathe. I think you owe it an apology. What is art.
Art grows from joy and sorrow. But mostly from sorrow.
It grows from human lives. - E. Munch

Love it when they are locked, absent and listen far away, no voice reaches.
Good days, best way to find out if you can trust someone, who you trust !

Adult education ! Strictly speaking, I don't drive a car
I would have to restrain myself from driving a woman,
that's in my ears while driving, opposites that are far apart
to try it with each other at the lowest point of one's existence
One portrays the part as unloved, helpless sexual object,
the other always waded through shit, even dropped off the child
and just as unreliable as your own mother.
But no one alone would know how reliable they have become,
like their own mother? As if I knew how long this would probably last?
One because of the gutter, always hurt in her pride,
the other had never learned to manage emotions,
Whenever there is a lack of understanding, she becomes hysterical,
as if the world around her would end. Both in a car Huahh Hahahaha
maybe manage to leave the city. From then on everyone goes their own way,
I swear, to put it formally.
PRINCIPLES; which disappear over the course of YEARS or MONTHS!

I also don't have the ambition to help those who fall short in love, who even without emotional intelligence make up for this predicament by tormenting another person in their nearby living area.

Mentally injured people without good examples, under supervised observation, already aged, they get hot, they get cold, who have a bleeding nose even at the sight of good people. It is their envy that others act in friendly exchanges, who have sympathy and empathy for what is at stake, who laugh with the other without missing anything.

Those who trust the medication that robs them of their vibration, they imagine, are exemplary limited, stuck people. If they were younger, they didn't have a childhood. Once they felt adulthood, it was perceived as a loss. The Party Lions' record is hung on the song without any significant knowledge, problematic, erotically out of line behind masks. To finally feel bigger, higher, further, by terrorizing those living below them, they should beg for peace, which the perpetrator never feels, but only has back pain, limbs as heavy as lead, the blood vessels in the legs are overloaded, weight gain just by thinking of food. Yes, the air under the hood is getting tight, not having any friends.

Even Jesus went on vacation, and the woman who stayed behind, begging for a spa, asking for Aunt Emma's cake, then Uncle George's cigar smoking, smoking the ashtray is out of the question for a German woman. Statistically, the app is for Looser, because she has already paid a fine for an administrative offense, paid off another reminder from the district court, but still confuses the harbor tour with the lack of awareness that her appearance would be as conspicuous and admirable as it was in her youth with enough extra make-up applied , compared to an Ikea scented candle in purple or turquoise, i.e. the Ikea inspired one of a lifelong marriage with its narcissistic reflection.

WHERE ARE THE PRINCIPLES??? THE PRINCIPLES ARE GONE!!
American wrong decision: the West, the war of aggression against Russia not countered, as the situation requires, that is Failure to provide assistance, old men whose deeds are missing, who act negligently,
inspired by the onlookers, that endanger the entire West,
the European Union of States, the democratic peace.

THE BIG SILENCE ! Mentalists work methodically as follows:
They gather followers, make them dependent on themselves
have pseudo-legal expertise, process of gathering information
Psychopath who wants to heal all of people's trauma
especially the naive ones, whose demons he wants to know
separate individuals from others like twins being together is declared bad
Gaining control by saying something, paying attention to where you react
emotionally, then working your way forward step by step.

They want to belong. You don't feel like you're part of this world.
They believe they are starving as orphans.
They ended up despondent in the ditch.
They would give everything they have for enlightenment.
They value friendship and are very loyal.
They have suffered in rage, anger and hatred.
They grew out of guilt, shame and fear.
They drink from the cup of death.
They dream of a new beginning in the name of the mentor.
They shine brightly in servitude to naive people.
From now on you live separate from the world.
They are responsible for the illusion that triggers are a sign from outside.
You're no longer sure what's happening.
They live out of fear of being alone and crossing boundaries.
You experience the thrill of torturing people in order to feel healthy.
They leave the middle and send you into the dead end.
Do I want to be happy? Like the punk at the main station?
Like a pig in a brothel?
Like the pug in the oat straw?
Like the one with the bow in the beer tent?
Like at the checkout at Mac Donalds?
Like the injection pump from the clinic?
Like the bright red one rising out of the tub?
Like the one with the most expensive sweater?
Like the choleric old woman in the library?

How do they believe in love eternity?

No, I really don't deserve that much luck.
Please carry on like this, you lucky little piglets!

If I went into politics...then not about me to expose 1000x to the lie,
that me populists hurt 1000x, then until I turn 76, and still cling to power,
because I demonstrate voluntarily, I don't give away a farthing, to the grave!
Officials do it in front of everyone, pretend to be blind, deaf and mute,
and shirk responsibility ! If I went into politics... then not to mince words !

If the UN is no more,
If Western politics no longer stands,
If the highest offices stand for nothing in terms of values,
If decision maker no longer have anyone standing...
they actually only belonged in a retirement home!

Take this advice from me: Don't let your wife name her first child and don't
ask me why...!!

Hahahaha, ... that's right! My child's name had the meaning
Everyone's in Julian, the July month, then I gave birth to him August,
the Jule time, Danish Christmas, the Jullien, the Juliane, the Jullienne,
Yay, what a versatile name, and I said to myself even if we do it with all
our hearts, accomplished alone for 17 years, whoever wants to get out there
too It can be ANYTHING! and that's how it was.

Cooking for him - in Germany ? You know that was a law
until 1997 saying, for the married couple shared "auxiliary apartment"
takes place - so translated - the sexual submission of the woman,
than that performed by the man over the woman Marriage duty !
That meant until the date the sooner one didn't "attend" church first place,
the more likely they were to avoid marital rape, casually mentioned, I also
gave birth in 1997, decided to parent rigorously and completely ALONE.

What did love do to me? A remnant left behind I no longer had eyes, ...
to see the guy's relatives from the whore line, I had no brain anymore, ...
noticing the guy's loss of brain matter, I had no ears, ...
because the illusion is like a bouquet of fragrant flowers,
which make no sound after withering,
that's what "love" makes of us, it's just "Itchy Passion!"

In the past, all Jews were chased out of the country. Today, since 1945
the chosen members of the family were hunted rigorously into the gutter,
beaten blue and green, with shame and disgrace, exiled never to return,
and chased through the country, if you reveal this to others, then denounced!
NAZI PERIOD AS PLEASURE!
So take your legs in your hands, and flee the BEAST!

The old farts … do you know them?
Those officially in power … who listens to them?
The teachers officials … what do they teach?
The music professors … how do you listen to them?
The clericals … Where are you headed?
The families without morals … Who do they sacrifice?
The people without names … where did they all come from?

I JUST SAY - HAVE A GOOD TRIP !
Well, yes the brave wise ones who love to travel so much,
with water bottle and sunglasses. It was once a Euro ticket from Dad.
Well, meet there in the desert those who chased them away
without water, shelter or morning coffee.
Well, you love standing there on the edge lets the hawk scream,
times away from the hustle and bustle.
Well, they were long forgotten, the ones you met at school
your leather football for everyone's amusement shot forcefully to forehead !
A joy is on my side. That I trust that disturbed me always will provide some
answers! That they have to give in when they realize their fears. That they
give me answers, which partly free them, in this way, end to the situation.

104

GOOD LUCK !
Everyone has lost something, maybe his child,
Maybe everyone was bad to him at some point. Afterward perceived,
everyone recognizes that you weren't a good father. Recognized from
somewhere, it probably shouldn't be. Some tired of life calls it clever,
perhaps to play the part of the madman, as if he wasn't alone.

As an educated and studied woman,
I'm going to give a damn, what a milky face hopes for,
how I would see myself as his wife. HAHAHAHA is normal.
This kind of nonsense started to happen in 1982!
When I saw the first sire just next to me, next to my mother,
and the dream couple had found each other forever.
As if I had to ask both of them, how their childhood and youth went....!
HAHAHAHAHA whatever, it's been too long now HUAH.

Who could we possibly find? who tells us that it happens quickly?
Who could we possibly find? who tells us that it wasn't cruel?
Who could it be, if not the child within yourself?
Who did it mean to, to TAKE the FIRST STEP?

FIRST HUMBUG: no one deflowered me,
because the stupid MASTER didn't even exist.
SECOND HUMBUG: Currently in FREEDOM,
it happened that the JUSTICE most recently in 1982 the lifelong
TOTAL DISCHARGE has abolished.
THIRD HUMBUG: that I will be in 2024 in 114 published books
proved on 23,500 pages, I escaped the family dungeon.
FOURTH HUMBUG:
that my son was born on the 11th like me on November 11th successful too,
1997 with intense contractions safe with me, to definitely RAISE ALONE !
in 1997 it was decided that "residency and marriage are no longer an
obligation through the use of force the woman to submit herself sexually to
her husband !" so church, do what you want, YOU WON'T GET US !

I agree with her who said that.
When I visited Israel at the age of 17,
There were the long years of the new war,
from the approaching border again,
When I heard both, and was a guest on both sides, ...
When I found out Israel was peaceful, and spoke to an old lady in 1982,
she drank tea with me, and I still miss her.
We talked about "Germany" and their experience in Auschwitz.
We looked at books together, and I also had my personal experience.
BAD experiences in my country.
Right at the beginning when I was back in the country.
I know the danger involved. When my friend there, who I met,
was still alive, she would be 120 years old now....

I would like to be a girl with my own horse.
It could take me far across the country's borders.
I would like to be a girl with houseplants.
Then I no longer had to spend time with visitors.
I would like to be a dog therapist.
I left the stupid donkey in the sand for 45 years.
I would like to be made for something bigger.
The one who allows ovulation will do it.
I would like to be a hobby Cristal Meth Power Point servant.
There on the screen you would have overlooked the fact
that I learned three professions.
I would like to be an artist with a stage name.
Then I can emphasize, teach people health.
I would like to be Fortuna from Saarland,
the bust in the garden waiting for me to replace it.
I would like the sausage on the bun to be made from country sausages.
Unfortunately they didn't have much of my presence there.

I would like to be the princess of the pony farm,
would jump over stop sign with the prince.
I would like to be the one with the roof of the world over my head.
But let's throw doubts into the wind, on the roof of the car.
I would have liked to perform in my pajamas with the music playing.
Afterwards we would eat spaghetti together at the round table.
I'd like to go drink some schnapps with fat Waldemar.
Because he has a sense of humor that not many who walk next to you have.
I would like to understand a lot more about life,
but I always should get drunk with them.
I would like to drive around Kölle like a fart in a taxi.
I wouldn't have noticed my crazy ideas.
I would like to sit on the street with all the children and joke.
But the mothers would laugh much louder, that wouldn't be allowed.
I would like to offer my friends something in Rockn'Roll,
saw them all flying by from the planet.
I would have liked to have had something like a home.
But the 7th heaven didn't exist this life!

DATING TRAP!

Completely private

One joy on my part is that I trust that those who are disturbed will always
provide me with a few answers! That they have to give in when they realize
their fears. That they give me answers that partly free them and in this way
put an end to the situation.

Good luck ! Everyone has lost something somewhere, maybe their child,
maybe everyone was bad to them at some point. Afterwards, everyone
realizes that you weren't a good father. Realized somewhere, it probably
wasn't meant to be. Someone who is tired of life calls it wise to perhaps play
the part of the madman, as if he were not alone.

If you had the people of Schleswig city
at that time... the highway wasn't built,
or instead in three places a raised moor was created,
then Schleswig would have today, more than just a bog body.
That's why you build around them the museum now for 45 million
a bit bigger, you never know, whether the future raised moor
don't show up unannounced still registered !

The market was great, we talked to our favorite friends and got what we
needed. Then we talked about backing off and not being amused, and then
said "thank you" for giving me the strawberries I had left, two bowls of
extra Strawberry Plus Ultra for half price just for me , and had given
information: "It's affordable if I save the thought of vegetables next time!"

The Nordic walk in the middle path.
The Nordic don't fall in others arms if just expected.
The Nordic stand straight at the traffic light.
The Nordic tell each other on all the ways have a good day, if they are
among friends.

I see the climate changing.
I see the divorce is going on via Cum Ex corrupt.
I see the Labor Minister seems to be worried at the moment
for especially the "unemployed", they are already starving,
but it is doubtful... in which direction this concerns,
there are actually women, men
the vast majority with all those who defame bullying
Coercive measures and authoritarian means
Job seekers work bans get granted, and look stupid !

I would like to say this to as many hateful faces on the street.....
You're the sad clown who cries, because everyone doesn't laugh.
You are in front of your dead audience almost booed.
You are the child that was never allowed to cry.

You're basically in the ghetto the biggest spaghetti eater,
but you never know how it came about?
You draw from Venice Carnival your grimace,
snap a second laugh, more a flash, a flash, without any thought.
Then a look to the side. As we know you,
in every street, how you always look around.
You start to descend, and so you end up getting further and further down.
The sad clown, who didn't make it, who never cries!

I have never Something was stolen, that's not true!
I looked good in many photos.
I learned about people.
I actually saw enough of men as a child.
I traded my choice to work for quitting.
I don't have a following, so I hardly have any visitors.
I don't believe in paranoid people whose fears turn into violence.
I didn't give a parade to my ex, I just broke up.
I don't have to shower every day, why should I?
I have beautiful breasts, still firm and round to look at.
I consider police officers to be upstanding, well-behaved people.

Good times go bye. To err is human.
Irish people are human. I don't know who I was anymore
before I knew this guy! He did bad things. But today he is different!
Since I love him, he has become completely different.
He's all too good for the world. That's why everyone wants him dead.
Let me be his sex bomb. I'll definitely make him happy with this.

Why do you assume that this is precisely when people miscredit foreigners
reject, disregard or scare away, who, even at home in bed, have no regular
change, no sexual experience, and feel new enrichment...?
You really want to know which cities in Germany had children's
concentration camps! Children's concentration camp – Schleswig
also called - Hesterberg - Home for orphans, foreigners and Jewish children.

Wedding and Bolognaise? Or don't get married and... Meatballs ?
Where do you live ? French fries or licorice?
Postcard or opposites? women and foreigners, are they the same minority?

Latest political discourse, Germany: basic child security comes,
only if they... SUV - traveling FDP members is paid out,
so that only children at all be conceived into this land,
it's not called that lately FOREIGNERS IN -
but pregnant with meaning FUCK AFD!
The aggression of the mother's son he goes as guardian of the law
including his formidable choice of words
into the cellar of his abysses, and tells his beloved,
"She has absolutely nothing she still has it SAUSAGE and MUSIC !"
from the bondage chair, so to speak, like prospect for everyone in poverty,...
SAUSAGE and MUSIC! until she agrees,
distributes a word to... a sick mother's son to take him as her husband !

I looked at the daisy in silence... I had removed the "Don't love me." and
thrown into the void. I kept the yes-I-love in the beating of my lips to plant
them in yours. The yes-he-loves-me remained in the sleeping silence of the
night and the one who doesn't love me. They sadly returned to my fingers...

Dvelling in the cave of the heart, the mind, without form, wanders far and
alone. Those who subdue this mind are liberated.
The mind without friends,
and the moon over his head,
the sun in his heart,
the love in his speech,
He wanders far and alone !

It's if different things happen, and you look ahead,
and you long for someone, and you are sure You are already there !
It can be seen ahead. It is often difficult to think clearly,
if the people that we love something happens.

A guarded mind brings happiness. Associate with the wise. Language is perfection of a mind, let the discerning man guard the mind, so difficult to detect and extremly subtle, seizing whatever it desires, a guarded mind brings happiness.

My words are not...KITTEN WILLOW !
My uterus no...MACHINE !
My will no...Bargain market !
My existence no...OBJECT OF VIEW !
My worry...no CRY FOR PITY !

SQUARING THE CIRCLE!
What potential for incest.
Two families in front of their children.
The children are all naked.
Offered blows to one.
That this is free to just feel naked.
One of the two mothers, so proud of herself.
She thought she would have been burned if she had been burned.
The sister of her brothers, the sister,
the tantalid curse of excluding the one.
So that everyone had something to laugh about.
Which is why the family feud makes sense.
Just so everyone knows what the Nazi orders,
They are all narcissists, but one is not.
Because she received no part in this squaring of a circle.

WE ARE ALL INTERCONNECTED !

I dreamed of a white beach with a man, whether it was you, and possibly it was my place of rescue, from where the shaman Lone Wolf was with me, and I was looking for a safe place to live in a house.

Sometimes it doesn't matter to me that we German women, who have suffered the most extreme violations of their human rights and are almost alone in their country, have to deal with the facts of their losses in life on our own, that it is assumed from abroad around the world that every one of us misfortune only happened, and that we were abused as a family, chased across the country, denied us papers, prevented us from voting, banned us from working, stole our children from our maternity beds and abused them in front of our eyes, raped us several times, banned us from the family worldwide, humiliated us, insulted us at every job, bullied us in training, excluded our children, but exploited our friendship, solidarity, power to help others, without an ounce of thanks or solidarity, neither an employment contract nor the promise of sincerity made true. But when old acquaintances spent our time living single, our principle of being single was broken in years of harassment that only aimed to shame us. Solving problems is something everyone has to recognize psychologically. Solve your problem by thinking clearly in order to solve the new problem as best as possible. But then the mother's sons and rip-offs used the networks to take me into their confidence in order to solve their own problems and to encourage me to give them everything. I could in the way of active participation and gifts, and to shame us again for being so stupid and naive to have been able to trust a foreigner. And it goes even further, these people, in whose friendship you were forced to stand by out of responsibility and sincerity, say it, to a grown woman like me, who is completely alone in my life, that my family should better not exist at all and that they all better not have been born from the mouth of an absolute mother's son who can't get anything done! Now should I also wish him a good night before God and express my gratitude for so much good will?

Should I say how one describes aging women, their hate on their bodies? The word designation also comes from sign, for example, when a person who is intolerable in the immediate vicinity, suffers from whatever mental illness, that they are considered intolerable! The term "she has the headache!" is striking! as red sponges appear on her face when she is forced to look people in the eye.

Buddhists would describe this as people having certain liver diseases that destroy their liver, as if an uncomfortable woman were always hunched over, carrying a trolley in her hand with a constant daily ration of canned beer in it, because these people hate them so much that their cheap behavior makes them uncomfortable destroys the liver. The doctors prescribe blood thinners for these women so that they notice that the moment someone actually looks them in the eye, their anger shoots out of their face like blood shooting out of their nose, and that's exactly how it happens.

Terrible and beautiful. Don't trigger your anger, and pass negative message on your brain.

Aging men become regardless of time
not necessarily nicer and not younger, but instead of smarter, stupider,
therefore they needed even more their therapists to stop them from
that they are those who are younger, more beautiful, smarter
something not given to everyone...officially decide to put a fist in it.
Alias Till Schweiger against Jan Böhmermann !

THE LITTLE PRINCE !
I'll be with him, don't talk about the weather anymore...
I didn't care about his weather stick all my life !
I wouldn't have any use either for his carving...not my dog would have any use of it ! I don't pay attention to his fake Santa Claus,
The one made of wood, as big as a DIN A4 book !
I shit on his little dick, which is supposedly made by children's hands !
I could puke, because he thought it possible the staff
Just offer it to the dog to bite !
I hardly pay any attention, that he picked up the broken branch
offers me as the beginning of all dreams !

Camping in Berlin doesn't have to be expensive!
It requires backyards, containers were used, or joins people.
Camping in Mecklenburg-Western Pomerania doesn't have to be expensive!

It just takes freaks, you used their construction trailers, or get into farming.
Camping in Hamburg doesn't have to be expensive!
You join in, or took advantage of the free pole dance show,
you already know where you belong...

If a murderer were to tell me that he needs me for something,
because I seemed so sociable, but he would tell his colleague friend,
miss the chance to apologize, because he truly loves his colleague,
I would notice how convincing the one as a guy rips off the other,
and leave the astonished naive, he brings love into the conversation.
If I noticed the heat on the gay man, the beauty at the edge of the pool well,
I don't know between fries or a surprise bag,
or to distinguish between mayonnaise or ketchup,
because I turned to polygamy, then I just left neither of them alone !
FACTS and DOUBTS ! What kind of cheap scam is this?

Things like that don't attract people !
If a women rapist who is as old as an old man,
makes himself important, So it really wants to be interesting
for women, its victims, on stage his little cock and complex
just drives up into politics, the worst ugliest bird of all?
What a sight this is whose children were fathered by the devil,
and gave the grandchildren to the devil?

Little blonde girl. Dreams so much about getting married.
You don't want to see your parents anymore.
Her tattoo like two arrows on her pussy. Career in the big city.
Lets you lower your gaze, look inside, hunter looks deep into her cleavage.
She thinks she's a flower which blushes in the afternoon and then
lowers her little head, closes her eyes, and until the next morning
the leaves close around the flower, and imagines, as long as eyes closed,
the evil eye never sees them, and she is very far away, Beautiful.
I just haven't had a big, strong wolf yet, who all always pass close by,
one with such thick strong arms for her, who replaces her father.

The Goddess of Love.
If everybody would have used preservation.
Climate Change would bring chaos. First Love wasn't as promised.
Given Existing not successful. Burnt finger with helpless ending.
Paid consequence for thoughtlesness.
Gratitude for savety in authoritarian system.
Awaiting what Big Bro shall say. Earth will come in the second step.
Then everything will drown fast !
...and if all this comes to pass,
...and contraception is obstructed,
...and free sex is banned,
then it would only have confirmed that JESUS would have come anyway !
THE GODDESS OF LOVE !

Jesus basically emerged, bound in foam,
and thrown away, as the German said,
who knows the do-it-yourself thing well.
You hardly know the German as being very widespread,
unless he flies to the moon, as unpopular as he is, so you hear.
The Pope bans condoms because he knows
that you can do without them, Even if Joseph had used condoms,
Jesus would have come anyway. Better safe than sorry, that's the German.
He uses condoms, she takes the pill, and they still sleep separately.
That's why people abroad think of us Germans as Bio Germans.
Even worse, they first list how many years
each foreigner has spent watching porn films,
and then the German should be allowed to make him/her healthy.
Tip for teenagers ! THE FIRST TIME!!!
Take the example of the STOP TURTLE that takes a long time,
first they have to take off their clothes,
unless someone SMART has put in 4 stupid screws!
Then take the turtles' age as an EXAMPLE, as we know,
they lived to a very old age, and their SEXUAL INTERCOURSE is known
to be much more intense and long-lasting in old age.

The next generation, in WWI and WWII
German women again take aim at WWIII?
Looks so tall, so mature from far !
no, I don't need to explain to anyone, we are prepared !!
no, first laugh at the woman and from afar
no, for the show the celebrity has to bow to that
no, the husband was already taken care of
no, why apologize
no, that's not a cowboy's style
no, he who carries his balls with pride
sends those who are still wet behind the ears first
he doesn't ask serious questions
he basically uses first names and always looks at the clock
he discovers a new love behind every summer
he catches glances and turns them away
he is probably messing with his relatives
no, he doesn't get warm with me in the summer
no, he doesn't know how to recite a bridge
no, he isn't surprised by my talents
no, he hesitates in his choice of words and wanders around
no, the ghost itself only thinks it will never commit itself
BUT it lets everything and everyone get hot
and sees them all running like blind people
just like an omelette in his pan,
and sticks a cheap little heart on everything and everything !

DIE NÄCHSTE GENERATION !

FAST PERFEKT VERLIEBT !

WWIII - Anyone who comes from outside and has an IDEA,
like our women in the Cold War... first impregnate them,
then leave them to sit, or...
then take the next most likely woman to their own country,
then leave them to sit in a brothel, or... then on the third attempt rape
the woman from the same family at 17, then make a run for it,
because martial law dismisses such things as trivial.
Everyone plays by their own rules, and no one follows national customs,
so if we are at WAR again, the whole game will start again,
and WOMEN be warned !

The best thing you can do for yourself is know your self worth. You deserve
more than you think. Always remember that. "How did I get myself into this
situation?' I repeatedly ask myself on a daily basis. It's amazing how many
emotions we can hide behind a smile. Everyone has a story, everyone has a
past. So before you judge a book by its cover, try reading a few pages first.
Who you are when your phone is on 1 % and you can't find your charger is
the real you.

Strictly speaking... the voluntary performance of sexual favors
is like an emotional breaking of earthly laws, high to being down to earth,
as guaranteed to be protective in its effect and contradiction as the parallel
between thinking, waiting, switching and laughing
to stop the torrent of crying ! Strictly missing sausages still in the fridge !
WE ARE ALL INTERCONNECTED !

I dreamed of a white beach with a man, whether it was you, and possibly it
was my place of rescue, from where the shaman Lone Wolf was with me,
and I was looking for a safe place to live in a house. Sometimes it doesn't
matter to me that we German women, who have suffered the most extreme
violations of their human rights and are almost alone in their country, have
to deal with the facts of their losses in life on our own, that it is assumed
from abroad around the world that every one of us misfortune only
happened, and that we were abused as a family, chased across the country.

And they denied us papers, prevented us from voting, banned us from working, stole our children from our maternity beds and abused them in front of our eyes, raped us several times, banned us from the family worldwide, humiliated us, insulted us at every job, bullied us in training, excluded our children, but exploited our friendship, solidarity, power to help others, without an ounce of thanks or solidarity, neither an employment contract nor the promise of sincerity made true. But when old acquaintances spent our time living single, our principle of being single was broken in years of harassment that only aimed to shame us. Solving problems is something everyone has to recognize psychologically. Solve your problem by thinking clearly in order to solve the new problem as best as possible. But then the mother's sons and rip-offs used the networks to take me into their confidence in order to solve their own problems and to encourage me to give them everything I could in the way of active participation and gifts, and to shame us again for being so stupid and naive to have been able to trust a foreigner. And it goes even further, these people, in whose friendship you were forced to stand by out of responsibility and sincerity, say it, to a grown woman like me, who is completely alone in my life, that my family should better not exist at all and that they all better not have been born from the mouth of an absolute mother's son who can't get anything done! Now should I also wish him a good night before God and express my gratitude for so much good will?

Should I say how one describes aging women, their hate on their bodies? The word designation also comes from sign, or sign, for example, when a person who is intolerable in the immediate vicinity, suffers from whatever mental illness, that they are considered intolerable! The term "she has the headache!" is striking! as red sponges appear on her face when she is forced to look people in the eye. Buddhists would describe this as people having certain liver diseases that destroy their liver, as if an uncomfortable woman were always hunched over, carrying a trolley in her hand with a constant daily ration of canned beer in it, because these people hate them so much that their cheap behavior makes them uncomfortable destroys the liver. The doctors prescribe blood thinners, so that they notice that the moment someone actually looks them in the eye, their anger shoots out of their face like blood shooting out of their nose, and that's exactly how it happens. Terrible and beautiful. Don't trigger your anger, and pass negative message on your brain.

If a woman, let's say 96 years old, admits that when she was young she had a husband who, as a criminal, called himself a "Nazi," there was no reason to be proud of it. If a daughter, because of that, did NOT father a CHILD with the father who had an EYE on her daughter, then it can be concluded that her child was not a "Nazi," she simply went away, was against the war, against her father and his companions. So there was no need for "love." There was no need for a child for the Führer and the Fatherland....

Fear of missing out - In love - Pregnant
Fooled - Impregnated – Alone, Do you think,
because you're pretty, girl, that someone in the holy land will take you to cloud nine as a raising father?
You'll never find out anything better anywhere else! Do you think, because you're pretty, girl, that you're an exception to everyone else?
And, in contrast, irreplaceable, when he just goes to get the newspaper that he's planning a future for you like your father because you're pretty?
Never let yourself be fooled with promises? Do you think,
because he's not talking about an unhappy relationship,
that he wants to enter the planet with you,
from which you will look at the earth? Where not even God is waiting
and no army of angels will take you in,
the very person who impregnates you will leave you sitting there !
Do you think, because you are pretty, silly, will to work is enough to dream?
They will welcome you pregnant with hatred. You are alone with this.
The hero on the next plane, probably even landed back with ex-girlfriend !
Do you think, because you are pretty, little mommy,
that everyone doesn't prefer to be alone with those known for a long time?
You haven't found out about the backgrounds of those who smile at you,
much less how profound their thoughts are.

I am going to tell
that I love not a single one,
but I love universally,
that is the fact to be,
the greed and ownership of heart
is the opposite
that is wannabe,
I am going to get used to it,
that letting go is the finest thing to do,
has that fine,
and that style of gentle beings, to let grow !

I hear the birds singing. That's life. Sun and the sky. Birds falling dead from
the sky. Breeze drifts. There's a cold chill. I better close the window. I feel
really blue.

NO - A rapist!
will never be a soft feminist
will never become a woman
will never relativize what he did

I know a term for...
a rapist as a sandwich or jam sandwich,
simply smashed into the scrap press,
when the small parts from the back of the car,
like a roll with sausage,
in which he was stuck, fall out,
the jam that was stuck in it runs down from the top of the perpetrator,
like a sauce, otherwise there is nothing left of him,
and he doesn't make a sound anymore.

"Lying Moon" - Upon a bridge of rot and dread, Sat a man with a drunken head, He raised his glass to the lying moon, And laughed beneath its ghostly croon. "Oh Moon, deceitful silver face," He slurred, lost in his own disgrace, "Tell me lies, grotesque and grand, To numb the truths I cannot stand." The moon grinned wide, a ghastly sight, Its nose grew long in the pale night, "Your wife, she dances with the dead," It whispered low, above his head.The man chuckled, a horrid sound, Feet swinging high above the ground, "Your lies, dear Moon, are sweet and sly, Pour me more, let truths all die." "Your mother's bones knit this wood, "The moon intoned, as only it could, With every lie, its nose grew long, A sinister, mocking, eerie song. The man raised his glass, a toast to doom, "To you, my dear, my lying moon, For truth is dull, but lies are bright, They make me glow in this dark night." With that he drank, his final breath, A toast to lies, a dance with death, The moon looked down, a sinister grin,Another soul ensnared in sin. So beware the moon, that silver liar, Its nose grows long, its price is dire, For those who drink beneath its light, Are lost forever to the night.
- A. Duchene -

Trauma ! Driven into a corner.
Stayed alone in the room. No vacation at the caravan.
Head as big as a house. No longer at home here.
Oh, if only I had never come back here. No pictures, just a figure flying.
Whose cat faces are many. Who mimic cats. Who spit like llamas.
Whose eyes are as narrow as slits. Who smell like pigs in an army.
Who stink like foxes.
Who have giant ears. and sniff to get something out of you!

The feet are so swollen. The liver is swollen. The heart is a bitter almond.
Back pain and vaginas. Dark chest and tension. Credibility vomited up.
Smell in the throat like canned beer. Hands brittle like twigs.
The floor is covered with bird corpses. A bed full of blood.
Strange gestures when entering. Seeing eyes inside and outside.
The pancake on the face. The sky up to the stars.
The roof just flew away. The wind blows coolly over it.

A doctor who fails to uncover the mystery of how society is aging, where
the rising numbers come from, and how it happens, what the reasons are,
I'm just saying bad breath and what comes out of it... that people are
becoming immobile, that there is no money for care, that their cognitive
balance and multiple disabilities increase as they get older?

Imagine ... one
desolate distracted robot, with Burn Out,
exing a wodka bottle in 2 Seconds,
loosing digital functions, forgetting the past,
missing relationship, asit the evening in front of TV,
hanging in deepness, sadness
and silence ....

The citizen as a guinea pig...
it is said, "It would be a test to find out how far one can go,
how great the capacity for suffering of the citizens of a country is!"

   –   so much for the trust of politicians in their voters.

If a political virgin "MARIA" likes to spend her speaking time
blathering on about the hygiene of her menstruation,
in other words, making her period the order of the day
and considering it more important than POLITICS,
she can, for all I care, even bleed loudly from her eyes, ...
that doesn't impress anyone either.

Wurst Behaviour...
when the very last of scum
wear the polo-shirt on shoulder
like a dog, wanting to come with
with the narcisst shout in group
all the elitist narcisst but in a group looking like
a bench of burgers with hot fat sausages.

"Sorry, dear Doctor ! This is my problem, that.... always when see people, they do ignore me !" The doc : "Next One, please !"

What does a devil do when he is in a room with two women arguing?
He sits quietly in the corner studies. No space for violence against women !

Rock for democracy ! We saw you ! We are diversity !
Optimismus nur bei der Option - Demokratie !
Expertism - Weiterwursteln - systemischer Protest
auf der Baustelle fehlt oftmals einfache Antwort
Wie lernen Bürger sich selbst Gesetze zu machen ?
weil alle gleich und frei sind bestimmen alle
größere Wahlbeteiligung bessere Zukunft, Interessen wecken
Modernisierung nur durch Integration
lernfähig sein, sich bilden, mit machen können
Wissen über Rechtsstaatlichkeit
Wissen über Sozialstaatsprinzip
Wissen über Gewaltenteilung
Demonstrationsrecht, Alle Menschen haben die gleichen Rechte
streitbare Öffentlichkeit, Pluralismus und Grundgesetz, Konstitution to Go !

Optimism only in the option - democracy!
Expertism - muddling along - systemic protest
Simple answers are often missing on the construction site
How do citizens learn to make their own laws?
Because everyone is equal and free, everyone decides
Greater voter turnout, better future, Arouse interests
Modernization only through integration
Be able to learn, educate yourself, be able to participate
Knowledge of the rule of law
Knowledge of the welfare state principle
Knowledge of the separation of powers
Right to demonstrate. All people have the same rights.
Combative public. Pluralism and the Basic Law. Constitution to go !

Of all diagnoses, "normality" is the most serious because it leaves no hope........ - Jacques Lacan -

Yes, that is the wonder of all trees, each one is individual and shows how growth happens to him, like those old people with arms like branches, who hold even those Oldebørn, and reach out for the friends as well, and take a look who needed them the most. Trees know from the wonder inside yourself, this wisdom they share when express them. That's why the have a good look on you the wanderer to protect that lonely one.

Is cooking really pure joy of life?
We all like to open cans. We heat up something that is already seasoned in the microwave. We sizzle and add anything that tastes strong. It just has to be salty, sweet and fatty and boost each other's taste. But the fact that people actually spend TRIPLE TIMES as much on this convenience food, like less food with a super filling effect because it's nutritious???

Since i know that white bread is the death to the intestine, i never decided to buy that, just for fun few rolls once in a while. Have you heard that the poisoning and destroying of sugar some tell is more dangerous to our body functions than alcohol ? Avoid sugar as much as possible ! You see the liver gets fatted, the poison no more is sended out then to the bladder, then the intestine gets slower until its death, and finds no more function to keep the good stoff inside the body, the small veins get fatted, and the heart, brain, intestine and lymhsystem breaks all down, when the small ways block. Then those sugar addicted, as well as alcohol addicted and smokers or fat addicted do the same to feed the body with fat, that all once get stuck in the veins, and organs fall out, and you even may truly say to these poor fat people, that then would starve to death and get bigger with it. They don't want to hear it. Those sick people end as a trash can, all poison finds its way in, and nothing left it anymore, no good stoffs enter anymore, and it is a slowly death.

I saw a single walking mother today with her baby in her cart, she seemed to be of an age a little too young to be a mother, so about 18 years old, and she was fat like a hippo, and when I saw her again later, she was walking up the soft path for about 100m, she was almost hanging on the ground and couldn't push her cart, she looked like an old person who couldn't move or breathe anymore. That is sad. This is more the tip from me not searching for yourself, Be yourself !

Can you differenciate between the experience, after have had the dinner, and then say what you exactly feel, about being real fed, and heavy and filled like the mave of a goat with four times meat .... or more the feeling like have eaten one single small anything and be sure to stay fed the rest of next six hours for guarantee, not heavy but fed with power ?

A really bad man once said looking at his daughter,
who never liked him, did not need him,
did not value him,
did not respect him,
did not honor him,
when her father did not want him,
when she lay naked and beaten in front of him,
"WHAT A WASTE!"

A really brave daughter once said in her father's hatred
she did not see her purpose in life, she simply walked away,
he still has the club on his head, which she herself openly threw at his skull,
and laughed at the bungler, in front of others, because it was enough
gave way to blows and silence, was against the war, against her father,
was against the others, the taboo, and his companions.
So there was no need for "love".
There is no need for a child for a leader and a fatherland....
Her child does not want to have anything to do with any of them.

Success isn't how far you got, but the distance you traveled from where you started.

Because of the silence.
Life is fleeting. Money will win.
If no one helps you, silence helps.
Balm where no men live.
Because of the herbs in the garden.
The poisons work in 12 hours.
Detoxification by Detox is on everyone's lips.
Football results are making the rounds.
Miracles happen again and again.
No songs are sung about them.
Strange views from the roof.
The monastery gives the impression of its former glory.
But the walls are crumbling.
The stocks are doing badly.
The roof has collapsed.
In writing, they are bankrupt.
Don't use Barbara's singing,
because there are skeletons in the closet.

Some are destined to succeed, some are determined to succeed.
Anyone who wants to go to church with me once,
wants to get married and to celebrate
all those who are tired come to me,
for the digging party that lasts three days,
if you are afterwards laden with potato salad,
I want to refresh you,
the long journey from the country to the city,
away with all kinds of allergies and yet,
the best medicine...
then we will simply continue the digging party !

Let's look at it this way ten little football players,
the last one is hindered has to go into the goal,
shows no footwork, stands there with his legs apart,
lets him in, no matter, had fun,
that's how a child is born, the fan club has one more member,
that goes in well, Oh great, it could be that he has a nice old lady,
she takes care of it, whatever the last one enjoys,
the ball didn't go to head, but it was a goal !

Did you sign? You got through a crowd in the middle of Madrid
showed 100 children your open shirt, and bills in your pants,
whoever fell for their orphans scam, the "come in my boat"
had the "goddess Diana" put a stamp on them brother "Hagen"
you are hereby a victim of a scam, you have fallen for your simplicity,
come to meet me again, and I would know his name,
what he does, how he lives, where he is going...

I am a lonely runner. But a long-distance runner. Louise Bourgeois
*25.12.1911 – 31.5.2010 I am interested in overcoming fear. I do not forgive
and I do not forget. That is the motto that feeds my work.

He always wanted to be a crab, he is still sad have no scorpio sting, hungry
but all feet step in emptiness, his big wish to be big with big feet. No
guessing, abandoned kids, crab next door, his new love. He can't count how
to dance on eight legs, i would call "The One lost his number" ! Hitler dead,
May 30, 1945 ! His Nazi way of life over, that's what cowards did !

A blue tarantula ! The sympathy of spider, the long-distance runner !
To me is his many tryings in life, steady on the move, takes one step and
another step, never wins or looses weight, but staying on and on, never
pushes nor hurts one. Very careful soft creatures ! I would love to see
tarantulas as big as houses, as slow as a flower in the wind, as soft touching
grounds like earth, no more street, no more cement, we wondered, and
walked between their legs, and would thank for their protection.

The spider. She is like a Mom. Not many words. But caring with all arms. I lived without protection. Those who did that, came in dreams. Real people but just helping in dreamseries. In Reality they never did. Like the big blue planet earth i dreamed, to see that i am one child of earth, with the wish to once find my place, the blue spider so is a huge universe.
The blue of the planet. The motherly arms.
The guarantee that existing for all orphans.

Was one of the guys from school
a room next door from the boys' class
hardly any girls with the old teachers
hardly an intelligent village idiot
who invited me for a beer, parents on vacation as he said
his DNA lying in wait locally
his dog watchful
his knife at my throat
his parents' bed, and raped me when I was seventeen,
barely taken seriously, nobody listened to me,
NOBODY !

ProPublica is a nonprofit newsroom that investigates abuses of power. Sign up to receive our biggest stories as soon as they're published.

Nine witnesses in the criminal cases against former President Donald Trump have received significant financial benefits, including large raises from his campaign, severance packages, new jobs, and a grant of shares and cash from Trump's media company. The benefits have flowed from Trump's businesses and campaign committees, according to a ProPublica analysis of public disclosures, court records and securities filings. One campaign aide had his average monthly pay double, from $26,000 to $53,500. Another employee got a $2 million severance package barring him from voluntarily cooperating with law enforcement. And one of the campaign's top officials had her daughter hired onto the campaign staff, where she is now the fourth-highest-paid employee.

Get Our Top Investigations !

These pay increases and other benefits often came at delicate moments in the legal proceedings against Trump. One aide who was given a plum position on the board of Trump's social media company, for example, got the seat after he was subpoenaed but before he testified.

Significant changes to a staffer's work situation, such as bonuses, pay raises, firings or promotions, can be evidence of a crime if they come outside the normal course of business. To prove witness tampering, prosecutors would need to show that perks or punishments were intended to influence testimony.

Is there a stain on your trousers, like at the altar? Was it my luck, right there in the fattening farm, where my stain on my trousers came from?

Is it always the case that you carry on, even though the wall was there?

Is it only almost popular in this job, but where you are popular, your beer, they say, where hatred prevails?

Is it all forgotten that you were angry about?

Is the musician in you forgotten, what you once studied forgotten, as long as they kicked you in the ass?

Is it no longer possible to hear them say how stupid you are?

Is it the first car in bright red from the Auto-Mobil-Club-Electric-Company that almost drives over your feet and the child?

Is it their suspicion of how many lewd things you said and talked about sex? In the eyes of others, is your childhood a thorn in their side, that you are left alone with an unfulfilled love affair, like your car on the tracks?

Is it the unpleasant visitor, who always stays in the apartment
because he never learned to swim?

Is it instead of an inheritance in eternal wage labor,
that he has already turned renegade an hour before the wedding!

Is it the doctor who does not act when a serum works wonders?
But is it not her case to consider why someone has to die every day?

Is there not the light at the end of the tunnel? Is it not a guarantee
that your show does not promise the breakthrough to real success.
Ohh, no one in my life has ever just given me
apartment of 60-80 m².

Ohh, no one has just bought the apartment for me.

Ohh, no one has ever been able to confirm
the suspicion that I had ever been a babysitter
a child and a cat and a dog, that I was drunk at work,
or that I had put children in danger !
I must have been a big DISAPPOINTMENT for many people !

Example - housing shortage -
wealthy, solvent winners!
Example - skilled labor shortage -
choleric opportunists in employment!
Example - craftsmen wanted -
the foreman orders the idiots!
Example - tough but fair artists wanted -
the colorless expert is doing the performance today!
Example - participatory society is becoming stupider -
instead of singing along with one ear, singing along with the other!

Holiday Pic ! What about the own family ?

I tell you what .... do not raise children, even with the Biggest Dream,
you end in the One-Way-Street, of unknown people,
americans call that Gas-lighted, you might have even three kids,
and all three become damn ugly, then you dreamed of any Love,
one that you never knew for real, like a holiday under waterfall,
but what did you see .... at the end of the rope ?
You see on every pic with one kid, in front of the waterfall its thick head,
and the head bigger than any exotic view,
when you have triggered "Max nix !"and posting those pics
with putting some yellow emoji on their face.

RESPECT ! When did i get my first smartphone ?
- With 58 years old - and i had no damage done with it.

I drive a car.
I park and ride.
I lay down and the traffic.
I see the traffic light.
I show the parking easy.
I feel this.
I can see it.
I am coming.....
okay my parking lot i found
was the last one hour ago !

Tip for retailers! Cool thing!!
Good example from the USA!
Cooperative supermarket as a cooperative, for everyone
partial, voluntary work for a few permanent employees
cheap shopping for members

Then birds flew up as if sparkling, I followed them with my eyes, saw how
they rose in one breath, until I no longer believed that they were rising, but
that I was falling ... - Franz Kafka -

My friends !
He is young studied and medic, and we had a fight about diagnosis, and how to treat people, and the theme about rapists, and respect, then he wanted me to learn to forgive, not to fall in depression. I have enough mental power, not to fail with this. I am not falling. Such an event in my life, did not bring me off from a lifelong democrate level, and I insist on all respect to women !

Rapist, drunks, dealer, wannabee, unserious, who married us to leave her behind pregnant, or anywhere in the dust. These guys will not be voted by women ! IN ALL POINTS GUILTY !

The little guy with the trousers on,
not tall, but with delusions of grandeur,
he had a belly and small balls,
but two shoulders wide,
hardly any hair, but look, he had a tight butt on his body,
he wanted to train like that until he was sixty,
carried his tin drum around town
from a young age, but always alone,
and he was never good enough to join the marching band.

First of all, let's be clear...
for me the term "hobby horsing" probably means something like,
your dad is behind you at all times like a big, round curse
you are embraced by his customer,
you run around like his horse
you would never escape the carousel,
you are not happy about the circus,
you are his horse, his hobby,
the furry animal you can cuddle to death, there is never you,
there is only him, who does everything for you,
and knows better, and well, his hobby "make my horse!" but that only means you, that is the DADDY - CURSE ! You cannot escape it.

100% I insist that I did not do a compulsory internship!
200% I assure you that I would have laughed myself to death before that !
300% I can tell you that I never belonged to the middle class!
400% I was a masseur, a nursing assistant, a secretary's assistant, a single-parent educator, a horse farmer's assistant, a sporty person, a harvest assistant, a cleaning assistant, a cook, a carer for the disabled, a writer, an artist and all that !

But no one ever liked me ! I was overqualified and far too nice !
Judo, Yoga and Karate made me laugh !

i thought about America in few cases, there are 350 million people, in the land of the Free and Wild, there might be about 40 million kids, and about 100 million elderly, and about 70 million single households, then there are left about 50 million sick and addicted, then there are left only about 50 million married in family or less. Think about it then, that students in America are only the rich families, with money for student life, no more Native Indians, no more Poor with stipendia, and no more Dark skinned, who from now on will not enter in a free study anymore, so the masses of all workers and married and familiar people are dump and unstudied people without any interest in politic or the real news. Those people are the typical Americans who seem to believe that USA is a round plate and all others are easy to kill, or abuse or make wars, and cheat, because they were not the chosen folks of USA, they let all other countrys bleed for their own profite, and friends as long as they are good enough and in princip once after a while let the friends fall like the socalled german potatoe. Then think about the violence. The most study of an american person is in porn films, and horrific war games, and weapons. Then the developping seen from science said, that the body index of americans change to sick physic, and they get smaller brains meanwhile. Then think further. These sicker, stupid masses without any intellectual interest but a lot of violence in their minds, may once not only kill an innocent person for only 20 bucks in the pockets, but they could now kill a person for just the thought in his mind ! This is the fore going step to a new Civil War, and frightening.

Jo and i thought today if it was a good idea to bring out again a book translated in english, not the whole thing in german, but the essence of it in english, but i don't know if there is anybody out there thinking and speaking motherly english, that any time would take his time to read ? I just made the cover - in the german edition will appear tomorrow it much of it describing in all details the humans those i met and got to know, in man and those i know really, in women who suffered from the man in many cases, in women with their faults, too, it is almost a describe of all humanity of today and their change into such unhuman creatures. Sweden , Scotland , Canada and Norway are my lifelong echoes that i get, you see the people from Africa somewhere out there or from Australia, Japan or anywhere so far those ones share spontaneous respect, acceptance and kindfulness. From America not so many. They love all turn into ghosts, dream of a Big BIG and GOOD OLD Joint !

I am looking for protection by lawyer.
I am waiting for prosperity financially.
I am searching for serenity to fight in dilligence.
I am deciding to connect my strength.
I am pretty building my sexuality.
I am raising my wisdom.

I see. Those Irish or Scottish or Cymri or Welsh or World travellers
I love them, too !
They are like Sunflowers with the taste of Honey
and lovely beings with names of Flowers, I see them like Sun Children
they give and send the Sun to everyone, and recieve the Sun back again !

I'm watching a film about an intelligent young man with a cleft palate, but he wants to use his intelligence, wit and charm to make his girlfriend the woman of his heart. The film is set in the old days, when nothing was given to you anyway. Almost like today.

Dancing - the vertical way
to give your eyes stylish eyes,
standing upright to passion,
instead of lying down
and giving in to sexual desire,
convincing your chosen partner
that there should only be him,
because he fits in with daddy's plan,
because his wallet is full,
because his status makes it possible,
because it eliminates the competition,
she knocks him down with the club,
she says "Look into my eyes, little one !"
she would simply kill for that !

You like sitting, Madame !

You eat chocolate in public,
tear open bags of biscuits,
talk about cake parties,
demonstrate while chewing,
instead of giving others,
the half-raw neck steak,
teach everyone in all openness...
"Look how easy that is, how easy it is
to judge others based on something they can't do,
because they don't fit into your concept...!"

When I was young, I had been given a black hat in a pub and when I saw a
beer standing there in front of me, I laughed until I cried. Just the thought of
a twitching intellectual with glasses sitting there in front of me on the
balcony, who was starting to dance as if she could dance in front of the
camera... I couldn't have said it better, I wouldn't have wanted to climb the
stairs to her !

Dance, dance
let him beat,
not for the mean-spirited,
you rise on your feet,
like a stick of dynamite,
but only the one in his pants shakes,
and once you had made them happy,
all the lonely ladies,
today a hug is enough,
they fought,
they made up again,
in grass skirts on the boards
in ballet that mean the world,
in competition, who would be seen first,
and NOBODY wanted to know!

Selling land ist the deed
of people who search for this
what made their personality,
they want to be back in cave,
they lost their own,
so they want to own,
all that comes,
and business as symbol
for their lost souls.
When they move in their caves,
those they have stolen mother earth,
then they are forced to confront
confront their fears,
and get mad with it.

I know the rich people steal land
like small sick people
steal the house freedom
both want others to flee !

So why then a guy nowadays seems again still the same problems, for his
look like ? I was watching a film about an intelligent young man with a cleft
palate, but he wants to use his intelligence, wit and charm to make his
girlfriend the woman of his heart. The film is set in the old days, when
nothing was given to you anyway. Almost like today. The film showed him
bullied all around the way, then at least the fine, pretty, soft, lovely angel
girl from rich family was forbidden to marry such a guy she loved, for him
looking like this and not being well rich. She just took one from her level
and fell with another in love, as if love was a new pants to wear.

The streets at night.
Dim light from the window.
Barricades at the intersection.
Barricades around a construction site.
The traffic lights are out of order.
No pedestrians.
Young people roam through alleys.
The wind blows through trees.
Smell of garbage.
A wild boar roams through bushes.
A fox runs across the path.
Rats scurry along the walls of houses.
A broken wine bottle.
The alcohol licked up by a dog.
Bats fly in from the park.
The full moon is large and round.
Children sleep and dream of the miracle.

How do people grow old here?
Do we get together when we get older?
Do we share the house, what more could we want?
Old people know their limits.
They know where they are going.
They also want to die when the time comes.
They recognize it when the gods call them to them.

"Cooperatives" don't deny anything
they just need helpers who can do something practical
understand a professional trade someone can live for that
it's not about sympathy, it's not about proving friendship
nobody has to be special, but they can do their part by clearing out
keeping the house running !

Imagine one...old and out, the married in divorce, the unhappy
won't get younger, the young one passes, to manipulate and abuse,
this brick the small option between new hope and fall, surpressed him after
let his love fall so damn hard, Imagine one...whose life sense is over,
whose hope to a young love, whose blame and abused feeling,
Imagine one...failed in love this way, HE KILLS THE ONE !

Goddeste the last night was again one calm night and spend in savety,
sothen i woke like have almost slept and got back my usual peace and force.
That feels after long time fight for night peace like i wake then very heavy,
and my head is filled with soft clouds. But you know meanwhile these few
days calm in here in the house will only last for that time the terrorist lady
from upper there decides to give, then suddenly she starts all over again,
until all will be done to stop her. That is her sickness, will never stop her.
Sothen i must continue with a lawyer, and the landlord and might be some
carers to talk to, or this nightmare continues until our time of life ends. To a
sick lady is not the wording a reason to understand, her communication is
noises filled with hate. This i why my lawyer might maybe call me Monday
back for a talk about a strategy. This is a guarantee.

I have this problem now nine years, i see my dog protected me so damn hard, just did not want to know how fast my own son, if he would have moved in here together, would have gone grazy and ended helpless in madness or anything ! I mean the grazy people did force us to move before ! That is why i do not run away anymore, it was enough anyway all, you can hunt people only to the edge, but once it stops. You see now my Art to wording and make Art all kind, did study me well, to use the Art for Self defense, this all now lies in my voice, and i may raise this from heart. I have internalized the Selfdefense Aikido that i did for years.

So okay, Good night, friend.
A financial company needs representatives
to represent the secondary education
that the stupid people who otherwise would not have decided
to have an unnecessary insurance policy
that rips people off in the small print
so says the finance minister, who likes to enrich himself,
at the expense of the poor stupid people.
HE MUST KNOW !

Anyone who goes so far as to claim, as a white person, that they walked from the south of Africa to here, to wrest the father's child from the country where he died, to take him far away to the far north, and even there pretend to be a false aunt, that the little boy himself is to blame, that he lost his father in the desert, and is therefore far away among white people, defenseless, without the strength of his mother, his fatherland, only having to eat insects and vegetables, and perishing from defenselessness.... I bet this child is one of the MANY today, who are denied protection, who are denied educational responsibility, who also not received solidarity from the motherland, which has been placed in the middle, who is denied the necessary help, to show the world and to abuse it to show that a child is no good in the white world. This is ultimately negligent, as is the compulsive attempt to convince a world of witnesses of their GODLESSNESS, THEY COULD HAVE INTERVENED.

If a child is already committed to become a refugee, for life,
with only one chance to live, not to deny a world from which he comes,
and to live in a world to be accepted by them,
this child must become strong, and if made strong,
he would be able to survive here!
This strong child has the chance despite refugee status to become a king !

Sweet tooths trigger aggression.
Good-for-nothings never go out together.
Fetish is like the zero diet of ethical people.
I could puke when I have to hear about dieters.
The choice is always the one who stands for personal freedom.
Leaving the choice alive does not mean eating up everything
that guarantees the survival of all of you !

ICE CREAM HALLALI
Who is running along there, the prince?
Instead of dancing fighting for a good match.
Ah, off to the hotel it's hard to hold back, right?
It's served, and often the bride is dumped too,
puking like that in front of the stairs in the studio.
The puddle of vomit continues, runs all the way to the pharmacy,
so sleep through the women's allergies!
Once around the corner to the bar,
or to the pub for a beer, until you're tipsy, next please!
The piglet ends up on the compost heap.

My vision told me, that I am not reacting back to that sick damn lady in her
aggressive way ! I am not. I am not responsible to solve her own problem.
Anxiety is leaving my body. Sure, tears could be happy. But smiles could
also be sad.

Aging is like climbing a mountain; as you climb, your strength wanes, but
your view is freer, wider and more relaxed. - Ingmar Bergman -

We can conclude that the good among the persecuted are not highlighted. The bad in the church, who should really start running before the law or serve their sentence, are so internationally mean to children that no single country can be blamed. Good refugees are active, they perform and keep themselves sober, and they raise their children well. According to the office, the priest cannot be reprimanded at all for the beatings and abuse he maliciously inflicted on children.

Why is it that most people think that the presence of the elderly is a relief to age better, like in S-weden, S-witzerland, S-pain, S-aarland, S-icily, it just seems that way to them, strange that is exactly where people want to live... hahaha

Democracy is the best thing that could have happened to our country!
The wrong friends are people who you cannot ask for help in times of need because they are no longer friends.

Our people and medicine -
in the female belief, women are soaked in painkillers,
so they don't feel anything, everything is manageable,
there is always enough of it in the house,
only afterwards do they realise that freedom from pain
is their will, tradition, is easily predictable, CHEMISTRY among humans
is so miraculous and good, WOMEN'S RIGHTS small,
but protection from their menstruation, slightly incomprehensible,
that men don't have trousers, but women don't need them,
our country has a financial management with a business representative
after whom you can only kick downwards.

Family isn't always **blood**.
It's the people in **your life** who want you in **theirs**.
The ones who **accept you** for who you **are**.
The ones who would **do anything,**
to see you **smile,** and who **love you, no matter what**.

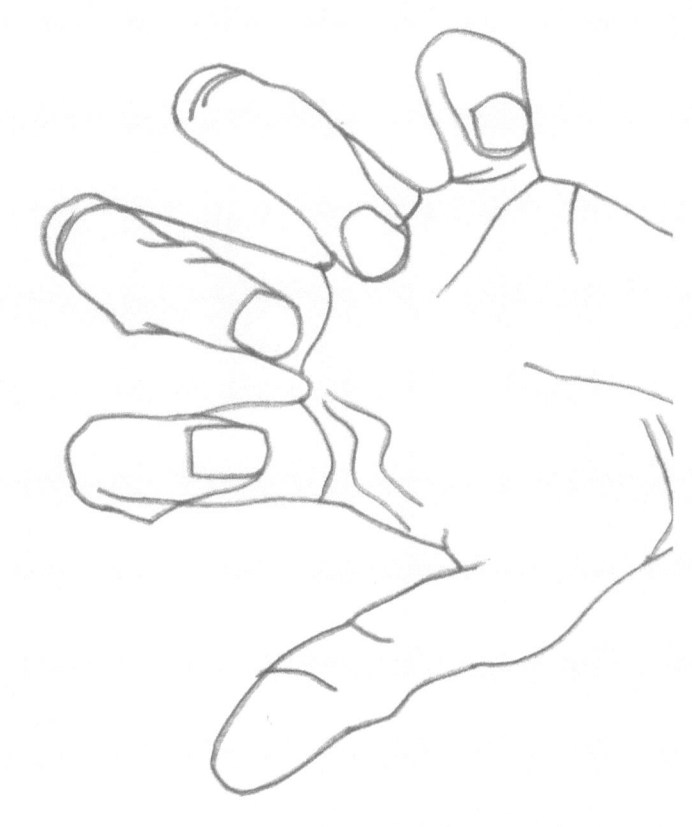

I dusted once.
It came back.
I am not falling for that again.

Where is the journey going ?
Reason kept
against or for ?

The strong being
Presence in use
shakes the story

Being as it is
for the better
castration in view

The feeling, your speaking
put on the wrong track
to be a stranger

Extreme reflection
shocking
smash ontology

The nature, because it's wild
should happen to them
they lust after that

Murder of reality
trace to the present
to destroy the future

Well 'see one'
but rather said
'I recognize'

Natural growth is a principle
of the spirit light
like that of the sun

The sense in the offense
in knowing ahead
to see the people

Nobody rises
in the light of the speech
it's just jewelry of rhetoric

The work of destruction
stewed cheese
blindfold

A story is coming
on soft feet
spirit riders repeat themselves

A hot iron
from the black age
still glowing in the oven

Loss of pride
daring gentlemen
who have failed

The helpless end
without any hair
it was to bend

Order to direct the worst case
in the full emptiness
is a vacuum

Thinking without morality
the goal future
without will – without arrogance

Check yourself
who throws the first stone
so animal–like a life

Passing away myth
to find oneself
divine and unflagged

Gentle being or
half of simplicity
to be a monster

A set of pictures
over it
evening sun wide sky

A pot of deeds
a little bit of will
arranged with diligence and luck

Virtue was behind the curtain
completed
which is not a vacuum

Look sideways
disguised dominance
to go to great

In dressing Ambition
the words
gives religious respect

Be a philanthropist
trade in being human
what friendship remains a trade

152

Tension by midday heat
remaining
a lapdog in his arms

True turns out
the skeptic wavers
completely lacks access

Valiant
come prepare
inventive the enmity

Connection
in bed
the other comes and goes

A self-experiment thwarted
neither reward nor growth
in the small glow

Gripped the soul
thus under construction
from the ugly to the beautiful

The soul is fighting
Lasting seconds
the trail creates a future

Effective up
resembles drowning
beauty in the essence

Upright mood in the picture
relatively risky
collected

Light uncreated
diamond shape
recognizable in God

Like pearls in the rain
looking for the ego
recognizable in non-light

Bending earth
a lifetime on the road
that awakens in the front

In the leap of the dragonfly
love yourself
Spirit as a cause

Nice is noticeable
love speaks truth
the goal is the good

To be the friend of man
to act automatically
The question is how ?

The marriage market
a vague promise
awareness excluded

Our people and medicine -
in the female belief, women are soaked in painkillers,
so they don't feel anything, everything is manageable,
there is always enough of it in the house,
only afterwards do they realise that freedom from pain
is their will, tradition, is easily predictable,
the CHEMISTRY among us humans is so miraculous and good,
WOMEN'S RIGHTS small, but protection from their menstruation,
slightly incomprehensible, that men don't have trousers,
but women don't need them, our country has a financial management
with a business representative after whom you can only kick downwards.

WELCOME TO DEMOCRACY!
The politician's business model consists of
1. high salary
2. obtaining money fraudulently
3. side jobs

political implementation -
ignores the wishes of the population as a whole and focuses more on the
minority of the rich clientele. The concerns achieved through referendums
can therefore still be ignored instead of being put into action. Women
seeking work, vulnerable children, and those who think differently are
attacked simply for being there. Trust is hardly ensured when those in top
positions come out as if they were autistic, laughing at people in need or
even concealing corruption. While the law fundamentally speaks of equality
before all, the rich are seen as less equal, which is what most of the
promises that are fulfilled tend to be. But poor people, who are less strongly
represented in the legal system, do not have the same lobby, and are
therefore punished more severely for minor offenses than serious criminals
from the upper class, who get better lawyers. There is an opinion mob on
both the right and the left that likes to pillory those who think differently,
with insults and calls for violence, in order to abuse freedom of opinion for
their own power and to restrict the freedom of others.

158

- **The best of me, I got from you.**
- **Mother is born from the connection to father.**
- **Character is invisible, but tangible.**
- **A man sees what he wants.**
- **If you want to have a say,
  you need someone to listen.**
- **You can only do what you know.**
- **Bandwidth is the measure of all things.**

Truth is often embarrassing.
If the rooster stands on the dung heap,
the weather will stay as it is.
- German astronaut -

Learn to laugh at your troubles
and you'll never run out of things to laugh at.
Hate is not the first enemy of love.
Fear is. It destroys your ability to trust.

Furies are loud. They call men a bulk discount.
Furies are deceitful. They don't look other special women in the eye.
Furies are made for men. After that they walk over dead bodies.
Furies only know bad weather, still stand with both feet in the dung heap.
Furies look around suspiciously. They always understand why it's raining.
Furies walk alone in the forest. They just don't know why.
That is their downfall.

That agreement of a witness
mentioned by the sick person terrorized,
have to wait and see whether the witness has the courage,
because it can all drag on,
the real hero turns out to be a friend,
not a simple man who just stands in the water
and goes fishing,
shows me strength and solidarity when I asked him for help.
It is common knowledge that all good friends,
even twenty years old,
ask for support in times of need and demand,
because they suddenly no longer know you.
first "I promise you, there is sun at the end of the road"
they say "I'm signing this for you out of solidarity"
at the end "I hope the traffic light doesn't stay red for much longer!"
Well, I'll just wait and see.
The lawyer also says I should wait and then get in touch
with her, no matter how, whether with a reliable word or not.

Thanxxx for all, i say, and tomorrow go to the lawyer, and then seem really
sunnier days come soon, even that this summer fell in rain, we have here 23
degrees warmth, the sick one up there, when she will find official orders to
behave calm, then she might finally think about it, wether to respect my life
under her, or leave.

Best wishes from Heike

He is the simple man.
He has accumulated extreme luxury.
His travel treasures are lying around.
His eyes dream of love.
His faith speaks of eternity.
The curtain separates from reality.
He likes beautiful and intelligent women.
How high he can fall.
If fate suggests that he could have murdered women.
It is not always the one who is convinced of his abilities,
the one who wants to make everyone believe,
if he didn't know them, showing that he "can" do something.

I asked her when Elves would rise
to help quell the rising tide
of darkness & maleficence,
the loss of heartful resonance ?

Her reply she cried:

"Creator knows where & when
hope to bring, Elves to send
Look within Sky & Tides
that mirror dreams inside"

Give the gift of your absence to those who do not appreciate or respect, your presence -The angel effect

If neurotic is wanting two mutually exclusive things at one and the same time, then I'm neurotic as hell. I'll be flying back and forth between one mutually exclusive thing and another for the rest of my days.
If we could spread Love as quickly as we spread hate and negativity, what an amazing world we would live in.
Silent disorder against the loudly proclaimed order.

Never be the level imitated, since it wasn't prevented ! Women have to learn to stay ahead, so it's taught, even if wounds still are bleeding,so none does dominate the helpless indeed.

To baffle your enemies, learn to tolerate opposing opinions. In the practice of tolerance one' s enemy is the best teacher. I will find you, because to confuse your enemies, to learn to tolerate conflicting opinions.
Worst enemy is always the one who understands ! I will find you - because it's amazing, how quickly your outlook on life changes when you have a child ! Truth is so, it will hurt everyone. It's about finding value for his suffering. Who heals is the one who keeps his knowledge for them wondering.

The planet does not need much more successful people. It needs peace-makers, healers, restorers, story-tellers and lovers! - Dalai Lama

There's no knowledge without risk. Risk-free life, however, does not have any awards. In a dangerous environment, you never meet many people! Today I'm warmly packed, there is a strong feeling that falls snow in south, but no one knows where it is going. All men have to die one day, but only a few learn to simply to live. Keep tears back, keep your smile, breathe and feel the river, clear thought, find your pain, stop in mourning, brush your hair and kiss the beauty ! Truth will hurt everyone. It is about finding value for his suffering. Who understands you is the only one who asks for your knowledge in solitude.

Solitude has its own very strange beauty.

The fotografer is hunting through room, skies and halls - The writer describes the feeling and bricks between ! Start by doing what is necessary; then do what is possible; and suddenly you are doing the impossible. The way someone treats you says, from what kind of person he is and not what kind of a person you are. An active ingredient readers need:texts that go over the eye directly into the bloodstream before they lay down in the brain. I'm an author! Last jerks! Even it's no room in the interstices for a quiet moment between things. Already the game is over my poet !
It's not about replacing that which is broken. It's about letting what's broken be shaped into something new. Things, you write to me, confuse my mind; you take me up to clouds, and you forget me there. take me back to your lap, be easy to understand. The role of a writer is not to say what we all can say, but what we are unable to say.

And of course, no matter how comfortable a perch we manage to bag ourselves, we are always a mere tug of the veil away from desaster, a split second, in which we don't look before stepping into the road, a phonecall away from learning, that we will never see a loved one again. What darkness. And yet into this darkness come tiny slivers and shards of light barely more than a glow it often seems, and yet somehow they help you to see the path ahead. For me those glimmers, have often come from books. A writer is not so much someone, who has something to say as he is someone, who has found a process, that will bring about new things he wouldn't have thought of, if he had not started to say them.

Courage = not the absence of fear,
but rather the judgment that something else is more important than fear.
Courage = pursue the passion against all resistance are the most fulfilled.

Read a good philosophy in the morning or before going to sleep ? Reading puts your head straight and keeps you grounded in what is really important. Keep smile. One day time will come, when they give up disappointing you. Certainly a writer only knows, what he thinks when he begins to read, what he wrote. That makes him really interesting.

This time my grandma died and I felt a strong motor to do something special, social or become a writer in a way, as if a book always slept in my heart. I detoxified my body, then I took a Poweralge from California - Afa Alge from the Klamath Lake and felt quite healthy and expressive for a long time. That is no joke, my brain started like a motorbike, almost like years meditation power and in every way. I've had a social year with the disabled and learned a lot from it. All professional care you give handicapped people, I think a lot more is needed, that it would comfort their lives. Unfortunately I was forced to give up work. In my office we gave people with disabilities places to work. I said that I wanted to work more and demanded better pay. I always tried hard to do my works to the fullest. Now I am a writer and a jogger and a painter sameway I am a convinced single who doesn't need to travel the whole world, because I found myself and all power comes from my heart. It does still make me happy !

My father,
the moon,
my mother,
who lives in it.
I became the one that none of them knows.
But that's a good thing !
hi, hello friend! Who knows where you are right now?
I've been very relaxed the last few days, even dreaming of my own mother living inside me, a beautiful blonde woman. She is always the same figure, a former neighbor. I felt like she had been adopted from my family all my life, but she still protects me to this day, warns me about others, explains other people's thoughts and intentions to me. She also shows me the family circumstances in which I grew up and how people have developed. This time she was blonde for once, but the same woman, and protected me again, warning me that if there was someone who was trying to hurt me, then I had a duty not to react in the same aggressive way, as long as our connection remains! I am very proud that many women meet me in dreams and praise me for every behavior I have shown.

I have a question. I have never been in a relationship with a man or a woman or anyone else. So I would like to know what someone thinks of me? Am I perhaps the ego type with a great need for patience, attention and care? Or am I seen as a transcendental magical sister who silently looks you in the eye when she has a wish? And who am I after sex? Could the other person be more interested in getting to know me once these first acts are over? And what about his or my dislikes, the lower tolerance for actions or reactions? Am I not a little too interested in all these topics in the whole world? If I am an open woman, is this man irritated by my jokes, desires and spontaneity, or is that the reason for leaving me from the start?

I think I know. I am the magically calmer type.

That's it for today,

have a good time, I'm going to prepare myself mentally for a really new good novel, I've wanted to do that for a long time. The lawyer, as usual, is now doing her part of the deal, and maybe I'll get some peace and quiet to paint again.

French people are not well treated, and get more and more desperate.
What will happen ? It is only one career that the wealthy French strive to get hold of a civil servant position through family relationships, and then spit on the proletariat all their life and leave them without a chance.
Riots, protests, violence. It is already working out. They have no chance outside these circles, they have got no schools for their kids, these kids live in slums and will never work and do just protest. And that state in France now tells, there was not enough money more to let social programs work for the youth, they just ripp them all off and let them fall.
As child i wanted to become french much, and travelled ten times to France, with lots of adventures and experience. Nowadays so...gangs and drugs. Widespread. Extremes of religions. Spreading people, who fall apart from democracy, distances grow, nationalism against women, racism, wants no elderly, no sexual freedom, no poorness.

Aggressive people, these people can be dangerous, but the most of them are driven by fears, so I see this is a pitty and they are helpless and more needed guidance, that made none really afraid, but people start to talk about such situations meeting them.

I had one long life, to work on my former experiences, and it took much strength to go through, but in connection to live on my own. And i know a partnership depends on both ones harmony. That is why i never tried it, today i feel like my fear really has left my physical remember. I can remember when my inner willing to heal, had a huge challenge to go through for more than ten years. With writing, meditating, sporting, walking, painting, breathing, calming, restoring, relaxing, working with my bones and body functions, Chakras, talking to people, because of insights while writing excessive much, communicating online, dreaming, and when my healing was growing then it was the time to let go my emotional world, then love feeling, while crying, letting go, then laughing me free for hours, shaking and shivering was felt so damn strong, that i once almost went to suicide, but my inner protection was strong meanwhile. Then i came back to harmony, and my inner worth, realized my personal quality, and good dreams came back to strengthen me, enlighted my days and nights.

Sure, I know that my rapist trauma will follow me the entire life, and flashes back seldom from time to time, what held me awake more than twenty years. I would love to calm that issue, i know about the better networking of brains withh the same working tachyonized afa-algae, helping me now for twenty years long, and I could set the start to many healing moments, what felt really good. But the best effect of medicinal plants and problems to be treated is the detoxifying effect, that are so much needed in this industrial poison we all do consume. I eat what i want, not living on a diet, because i suffered enough all my life, not to starve me, when i am hungry, that i eat what i am lusty. The hunger sometimes is like the earlier lust to love, so it is good to let go.

167

168

Anyone who loves his friends,
does not travel to the desert,
does not shit on others,
does not complain as a guest,
does not aspire to the highest offices,
does not cheat public money,
does laugh at all women,
does insist on the power of the church,
does not know what to do,
does not call others by their names,
does hobby horsing,
does it with one of his daughters,
does not show respect for their mischief,
does not make himself into a special being,
does not deserve any special status !

The guest is chosen, invite, inspire- is far more - than just choose the other proximity. I do not have to be patient with anyone, if I do not think it worth it. When i invite, then for a reason, then i offer my guest friendliness, my sexiness, questions to talk about and communicate, my taste of life to share, my path i went if it was good enough, my wiseness, my ability to give away. I found out my way to love, so then another wants to be affected, that's it. I am a warming heart, and the other wants to warm with it. I am standing and waiting until the visit finds time to arrive and eat. My calm and magic wants to give answers, and the visit finds himself in the speaking, that things long time not said have to come out, all those images shared about towns, and people in places, their sorrows, and plans and hopes.

I am a poor wayfaring stranger, while traveling through this world of woe, Yet there's no sickness, toil or danger, in that bright world to which I go.

We assert that we consist of atoms. I do not. We exist at all, then with the stories that we start in life ! Respecting life means to treat everyone well. Not exclusively those that you tried to impress ! Experience teaches vision to follow. Everything else step away. Living alone. Single parenthood. To work alone. Identify the core. Hunting for all beings - whether wolf - whether fish - whether woman is not sport, but it is murder ! It's just good to feel alive and to get it back, fall in love with someone as sweet as you are ! Bravely put on a heap of pebbles like on a little island, to dream a long and bright way and whish someone from there a wonderful day ! Not even more women are Saints today. Looking at them, see they run in sneakers, drink beer, suck at women's breasts and bark like dogs ... I'm feminine. That is like a child before the fire - vaguely smiling and tears in the eyes. In a giant landscape before me without dusk. I'm easy. A picture inside me. I am on a perceptible journey in the peace of my mind knowing it is all just one. To ask ? The communication in perception in the almost inaudible silence and response that gives everyone that nature that is not hidden. Real chaos comes from the garden of the soul, in which wild herbs grow.

The way to count on much experiences made me confident. MY life was a steady climb back on the horse that threw me in the dirt, and came back and again trying to hurt me with his feet. Men nowadays do own no worthy character, most neighbours are never worthy to talk about. Some wise people say, that the times we live in up till now, that is to be seen, that human has not such a strength anymore, and is becoming mental weaker, because his life energy fails more. So it is easy to be seen that the most with any life crisis end in medication, care and dependence of a bunch of doctors.

I mean it took years long to make my mind as young woman. I first fought and fell many times from horses, slapped by father, hated by sisters and rejected Mom, left alone, lost jobs, bullied in schools, living poor, chanceless with my son. But each time when staying strong in Every single situation to make all clear, can't harm me real, because their anger will hurt themselves ! And from each little lesson this made up to me, I grew stronger.

I am like a Big Horse, that had its life. To some I am gentle. For some I am desirable. For some, I am loved and versatile. For some, an inaccessible, distant dream. Flashed like a spark and disappeared.

Reality and fiction...feed and eat each other ! All fingers are not the same length. But when they bend, they all stand the same. Life becomes easier when we bend and adapt to all situations.

What if the many dissimilar people would bend together, we would become similar, we would adapt and adapt to each other ? Dream of locking yourself so that the interior remains accessible even after a long time ? We free ourselves and only then realize that there are others who feel the same way, then there are two of us after all. People, they go in circles and the boundaries become blurred - it's called mutual social manipulation !

Smoking Sage rituals help to break the ban, if you don't really know you imagine what ever better is !

Who desecrate women's bodies.
They chase the woman all over the world.
Then take away her self-determination.
The woman removes the child at birth.
The child is being abused and she has to watch.
Stealing the alliance from the woman and the child.
Then try to get her to thank you for it.
But they wanted to rent out their bodies.
But then they didn't earn a penny.
The two don't get along with anyone.
Both lives burned to ashes.
The country was deprived of human rights.
Putting the same suffering on the next woman.

Tonight I dreamed that Johnny Depp passed by in town, rushing through with me, and discussing why or how or if there are reasons to belong to each other as couple, but I agree, we were in a big hurry.

I think those insist on the theory of love, will never become mature.

Completely different from the original
I want to learn to fly young,
I want to love women because of that,
wander in free thoughts, see past in another world,
several times and in the cold standing,
wanting to get out to a better world,
which I left standing next to it, and continue to climb
into the distance walk alone in rocks, hike over mountains, and
really be alone that's what I stand for,
until I spread my wings free, and steals me into the air.

Everyone wants to fly !
No frame, unlimited, easy but don't offer anyone a smile,
Where does such lightness come from ? who didn't deserve empathy ?
Everyone wants from the lowest level be exalted, unconditionally,
where would you have been without any action ?
who makes a name for himself, so truthfully appointed poet,
to be invited to the blossom of a desert ? Everyone wants to be someone
else's lighting, but don't spend a night in the dark, where was the star in the
sky... to ask this for an invitation ?

Be guest everywhere in the world before !
Then invite the guest from everywhere.
Then offer your ability as Art and well known.
Then think about all again.
Then you might know about what you do.
The respect to your Art depends on how you are doing.

It's like good friends would say, I agree.
This is how I choose to live and not ask before telling anyone else what I
think clearly. So most people lose their suspicion as we talk and we end up
laughing. The guy with brain damage, I give him the compassion and let
him be and start to clarify, I accompany him through, even if I run the risk
that he will try the impending outbursts of rage, but did he understand it and
thanked me that. I was still alive, he had begun to live among people, not to
fight and trample them into dust and learn. The highest storms of love, and
then perhaps fall from heaven, has nothing to do with the man or woman's
position, everyone has these feelings. EGO soon rises to strive for the
achievements and recognition of physical body, thus undermining all efforts
to reconnect with the nothingness that it is, to connect and reconcile, for a
struggle-free existence "just as I am".
Telling stories is a favorite, not just telling people hard truths, women
looking for salvation, I made them all succeed. Imagination is the best way
to make people want to know more about the end of the story, all phases of
life to never give up hope and self-love.

174

"Children just hang around
There are worms in the flour, they ate the cocaine
then snorted the worms, become aggressive
today's kids don't need a high
but a fall from her high horse, no fumes, a damper
the prepotence and yet from Father a slap
But at least I haven't become a pervert." - Lisa Eckhart, my words

However I see it, who doesn't water the trees, does not reap any fruit, that's
one who is always escaping and looking for excuses,
will only experience loneliness.

Each business offering IS SUSPECT
they treat consumers online like childish idiots
be helplessly naive to believe in someone
any personal interest in all you do,
did or ever would do, dangerous !

I remember the last time I was in the woods
with those women, one really same intelligent like me,
she spoke about the same experience
a burglar who promised her anything to get money
English is the language for love whispers.

The mermaid jumps into every puddle
but does not pay attention to rough matchos
or he looks after all fur animals
thinks nothing of climbing mountains together
it has to look really good
that every hot soup turns cold against him
she likes to look for potatoes in the ground
the coast's natural resources are its quirks
she doesn't want to spoil her breasts
the north German Deern with a view of the wide
who likes to go swimming too much
but she is the fisherman's best friend
imagine them ... the hot mermaids
culinary delighted from going ashore
oppose her on hot raspberries, the hero
Spagetti in Cabanossi sauce with parmesan
means the selfish can stay at home !

AS SOON AS WE

REALIZE THAT IT's

Not OUR JOB TO BE

PERFECT, EVERYTHING

GETS EASIER AND

MORE HONEST AND

MORE TRUE AND IN

MY EXPERIENCE, IT

TENDS TO WORK BETTER

Who are you ?
Can't do anything and don't know anything ...
but wanted to be president ?
It would then be guaranteed out of thanks
create bridges for all of you existing artists
so that from now on you all together
have no school longer and hopefully
that you find yourself together again
and you will find shelter under these bridges !

Dear autocrat !
You are a deliberate, brutal murderer.
And You have murdered many.
You're a corrupt bastard. A manipulative carcass.
Your skin flakes are represented
right there behind your smile
the scum hides that you never wanted to admit !

I already had my sovereignty before the birth of my son, before I was a
mother ! I had language, travel, painting, imagination and a great desire to
have children. I have more the opinion that the type of guy like cowards
never confront with I close that these polygam blenders are "Childish"
take no responsibility to what broken hearts they left, they are tricky,
and that makes them dangerous ! They even leave children with a broken
heart in several types experienced abuse. The abuse takes over from one
generation to the next generation. They are no reliable friend, but well
known as the A-hole type. His only friends left him in a One-Way-Street.
The same way to end, where he left his broken loves. He would have to
think about his pimp behaviour afterwards, but while women spit on his
shoe, so the daughters.

Wealth and money do not confer power:

Power being behind to amass money is not meant to last. Take a look at the beautiful villages with the well-known, sought-after houses in the middle of the water, in beautiful nature, traditional and handed down for generations. However, it does not last in the long run if you consider how quickly people lose their wealth. For example, no children came or they migrated and never come back.
How quickly a whole family generation is lost and there are no more heirs. How quickly has someone miscalculated financially or has to sell the whole house when they divorce. People live as if there was an eternal future of prosperity and no politics or some other condition that could change the whole situation. It is illogical and not seen in real terms when people speak of power simply because they are doing everything in their power to increase their money. But for the sake of money they give up everything, do not live in a partnership, keep the truth at bay and keep people at a distance, leave no one around, lie and cheat and still do not do much more than see the fastest way that money will grow on its own. Cost what it may. Most prostitute themselves for this and do not even notice it. They even sell the soul and forego the experience of love even when it has screamed in their face.

Only later, usually much too late, do they get into the crisis, when they get the feeling that they are wasting their lifetime chance of knowing themselves for luxury. They hadn't cared about performing without bragging, but they weren't learning to leave something of value to the world. They did not have any children to whom they could add some human value to their lives. They usually realize too late when the screaming really starts that there is hardly any time left to penetrate from the surface to the depths or to become righteous. To do this, they would have to learn to give up polygamy, to be able to share, to make resonance to a friend, to look for competition in themselves, instead of making others their goal and wanting to improve. This is usually the main reason why such juppies need mid-life therapy.

Nur wer den Feind kennt
sein Atem und sein Herzschlag ist
kann ihn wehren.

Only those who know the enemy
is his breath and his heartbeat
can defend him.

When You admire something
about another Woman get into the habit
using real magic of lifting each other up
share different styles of accepting
different looks of believing that love is humanity
but not racism, decadence or hate !